C

CO-DEPARENT

NO MORE

****

Caring For Oneself While
Parenting Adult Children

****

Dr. Murphy C. Martin, LPC

CO-DEPARENT

NO MORE

Copyright 2013 by Murphy C. Martin

Library of Congress Cataloging-in-Publication Data is available through the Library of Congress.

ISBN -13: 978-0615781549
ISBN-10: 0615781543

All scripture quotations unless noted otherwise are taken from *The Amplified Bible* (Grand Rapids, MI: Zondervan Publishers, 1965)

Self -Published: Murphy C. Martin and Family
Po Box 931
McMinnville, TN 37110

Previously published as
Baby Boomers Self-Care/Parenting Book

Table of Contents

Dedications

This book is dedicated to the nation's first baby boomer, born just after midnight on January 1, 1946, and to the rest of the baby boomers - some 78 million born between 1946-1964.* Especially, am I dedicating this effort to those of us baby boomers or any parents who have troubled young adults whom we are trying to help as well as trying to care for ourselves.

Lastly, I want to dedicate this book in memory of my parents, Colson and Lavon Martin, who saw my brothers and me through some difficult days.

<u>Acknowledgements</u>

I would like to thank my wife, Dianne, and our four children for their support, encouragement, and participation in this particular six - year project. I also thank our children for working with us as we are trying to implement our own self-care while caring for and helping them in their problematic situations.

Special thanks to Marcy Martin, one of our daughters who typed and formatted this project as I tried to fine-tune what I hoped to accomplish in this book. Thanks to my sister-in-law, Peggy Hartline, for her help in editing. Also, thanks to Jana Barrett and Judy Walling for technical assistance.

We, as a family, hope our efforts will be helpful to all who read it.

The Reader's Page

This book is only one person's approach to a very large, complex and extremely important topic, and, therefore, embodies its strength and weakness. Its strength is that it's an effort born of experience to help us as parents of troubled young adults better care for ourselves while parenting our troubled grown children. Its weakness is that it is only one person's approach.

Since this approach is dynamic in that one can add to and take away from it as needed, conditional upon circumstances at any given time, I am suggesting that you, the reader, actively participate in both applying and modifying the various ideas as they relate to you and your particular situation. You will notice that periodically throughout this book some of the pages are blank so that you can add to, modify, or apply these ideas as you feel best suits the needs of you and your problematic grown children. I've simply called these blank pages – "The Reader's

Page". You are encouraged to read with pen in hand and interact as you tailor the ideas to fit your needs and apply "Boomercare" to your life.

Footnote: Also, for the reader's convenience on page 188 is a glossary of old and new terms (as used in this book).

Introduction

I have tried several times to write this book but cannot seem to contain my excitement and/or anxiety enough to do so. Now, here I sit at a bookstore, drinking a cup of hot coffee and waiting for my wife to finish shopping.

I have been interested in this specific subject for about 15 years now. There are three reasons for my interest: (1) My oldest child turned 18 about that time. (2) As a psychotherapist in private practice, I began counseling more and more parents with troubled young adults who reported increased stress due to this issue. (3) I hope this endeavor will be of help to those of us struggling to parent young adults who have serious problems in their lives...Okay, if I am truly honest, there is a fourth reason...I hope it's a big seller so I can pay off my house, a few other debts, and have a more leisure retirement. There, I said it!

If you have chosen to read this book, you know why such a book is necessary, right? There is a 'emotional pandemic' being experienced by us baby boomers and it is increasing at an alarming rate. We are trying to successfully parent our troubled young adults, over the age of 18, with not much help from anyone or anywhere. There is little literature written on this subject. Even the usual source of information for most of us these days, the Internet, with all its storehouse of knowledge and facts, has 'not much mail on this issue'. If you go to a bookstore and try to find helpful literature on parenting young adults, the best you may find is a few brief treatments concerning late teens or early adulthood. There are many books on parenting babies, but few limited offerings on helping baby boomers parent their problematic young adults. Not only is there little information found in the literature, I am aware of no research being conducted on the topic. Even though it takes a while for research studies to make it to the general public, there are few offerings to date for those of us in the professional arena. For example, there are no Continuing Education Units, no seminars, nor any informed dialogue going on in the academic community to offer much needed help.

Who would have ever thought that the 'magic, all-powerful' emancipating age of 18 that all teens long for would turn out to be the antithesis of emancipation for us parents?

Don't you remember hearing your teen, following a stressful difference of opinion with you, storm out of the room yelling, "I can't wait 'til I'm 18 so I can move out, be on my own, and do what I (not you) want to do!" Knowing through our own experiences that 18 was not some magic age of emancipation, but rather the age of additional responsibilities and expectations. We may even have had secret hopes that our teen's intentions would come to fruition and that their "independence" (emancipation) would translate into more time, energy and effort we could expend toward our own happiness.

This thought did not negate our need and desire to be supportive of their dreams and efforts throughout their journey toward independence. We did not realize then, in some cases (more often than not), the length and breadth of the path, where the journey would lead, nor how long that journey would last!

As responsible parents, the problem that confronts us is that we no longer have what we used to have... legal authority. Even though 18 is not the emotional nor relational emancipating age, it is in fact the legal emancipating age. Where we once had the 'power' to 'make' the child be responsible or accountable, on birthday 18, we can no longer productively nor successfully use the authoritarian concept to parent. To try and do so is damaging to the young adult, to us, and to our relationship with them.

No longer having the authority to 'get' them to live responsibly does not keep us from wanting them to have a happy life. We continue to love them more each day even though we sometimes feel helpless to 'get' them to make healthy decisions. When they do make healthy choices, we are pleased for them and for ourselves too! But, when they develop a pattern of making unhealthy decisions, we feel for them, worry about them, and feel unprepared to parent them.

It is hoped that my efforts in sharing a few thoughts on this subject will help enlighten and better prepare us in parenting young adults with problems in their lives, and also help us better care for ourselves.

Having said that, the model I am using to accomplish this I call, "Priming the Pump."

As a young boy growing up in north Florida, (by the way, home of the Fighting Gators!), I loved to spend time in the country at my maternal grandparents' home. Living next to them was a family who could not afford electricity and therefore had no running water. Instead, they had a hand water pump. In order to get the stream of water out of the well, they had to first pour water into the mouth of the pump to prime it before pulling the stream of fresh water out by pumping the handle up and down. Thus, what I'm trying to do is simply prime our pumps in order to help pull out of ourselves the fresh ideas that hopefully will work better than some other efforts have in the past. As some in the counseling field are fond of saying in referring to past failed efforts to do something, "How's that working for you?" So, if it is not working well, or at all, let me share with you as "...one beggar telling another beggar where bread might be found,"* some ideas, ways of thinking, attitudes, acting and relating, that might produce more positive results. Or, as John Claypool has worded it, my efforts are simply... "tracks of a fellow struggler."**

There are no quick fixes, magic pill, silver bullet, or right phrases that can resolve this serious and complicated concern. And, if you're like me, you are open to, and ready for, some assistance! Hopefully, what follows will be of help to us and our efforts to parent our struggling young adult while caring for ourselves and become co-deparents no more.

The Reader's Page

<u>The Reader's Page</u>

_____

_____

_____

_____

_____

_____

_____

_____

_____

_____

_____

_____

_____

_____

_____

_____

_____

_____

_____

_____

_____

_____

_____

_____

_____

_____

_____

_____

Chapter 1

The Problem

The issue seems to be that when our young adults have problems in their lives, are unhappy, act in unhealthy ways, and are irresponsible, we don't know how to help them or help ourselves in relation to them.

I've discovered that if we as parents of a troubled young adult with problems in their life are not careful, WE MIGHT NOT BE ANY HAPPIER THAN OUR UNHAPPIEST YOUNG ADULT! This of course can be a parent of any age child, but for younger age children we have many resources, from the *Bible* to Dr. Spock. And since the authoritative model is no longer operative, we are potentially dependent on the child for their happiness and our happiness as well.

Some would even advocate that we are supposed to base our peace of mind on the happiness of our young adult child if we are 'good' parents; that it is only right to limit our happiness to the happiness level of our children. To restate in psychological language, this is akin to being "fused or enmeshed" rather than being a good parent.

Of course, it is not humanly possible to be at peace as a parent when one of our children has serious problems, and I would question myself or any other parent who was so like-minded. However, for us to feel we have to live our lives so enmeshed, (entangled, fused, tied), with the child's that the quality of our own life is drastically effected by their pattern of poor choices, we essentially turn the table and make ourselves dependent on them for our own happiness.

What a strange twist this is! In the behavioral science field, this is known as a form of 'parentification'. What on the surface seems the right thing to do, when analyzed at a deeper level, is burdening an ill prepared young adult to make us happy. We are sending the message that, "If you are not okay, we cannot be okay either."

This dynamic is not limited to parenting young adults. It can begin early in a child's life with very unhealthy consequences, (but I'll leave this age group to the child and developmental practitioners).

Now, back to the thesis that it is not only possible, but also highly probable, that a parent of a young adult who has a pattern of irresponsibility might not be any happier than the unhappiest or the most problematic child. WHICH, BY THE WAY, IS A SURE SIGN THAT ONE IS A CO-DEPARENT!

<u>The Reader's Page</u>

Chapter 2

The Causes of the Problem

At least two dynamics seem to be the root cause for the above problem. One is what we don't have enough of, and the other is what we have too much of. We seem to lack a significant amount of personal autonomy and are much more codependent on our grown children than we like to admit. Ouch! The truth hurts! (At least it does me) These two dynamics taken together and in significant amounts can largely explain why we have so much trouble parenting and are so unprepared to deal with related issues and concerns. Ergo, we end up as, or even more, unhappy than the unhappiest child. This codependent phenomenon is the dynamic that contributes to years of unhappiness in extreme cases.

The dictionary defines autonomy as the ability to self-govern as opposed to being governed by another. Codependency is the concept where

23

two people each depend on the other in unhealthy ways. In many instances what seems to take place is the dependent parents have serious trouble self-governing. In making decisions as to their adult child, these parents are overly influenced by what the young adult is going to think of them and/or what the child is going to do, i.e., stop relating to them, not love them anymore, think they are bad parents, hurt themselves, etc.

What seems to be the reason so many of us have these two problems? First, the time in history in which we were born and grew up has a lot do with it. The baby boomer generation seems to be of a similar mind-set as to this aspect of parenting techniques and dynamics; more specifically, our having grown up during the era in which sensitivity to the needs of others was emphasized in a way that it had not been before.

During the 1960's, and with social programs making us more aware of individual rights of all people (including children), our society, our government, our religious institutions, our educational programs - all these and more - produced a climate of one's individual needs being important in ways not experienced heretofore.

This awareness began and continued to effect the way we parent our children.

We became not only overly sensitive to our own feelings as parents, but also overly sensitive to our children's feelings, needs, rights, and personhood! Combined with the fact that our young adults have grown up benefiting from and claiming their rights as equals, sets up the environment for the difficulties we have in parenting. In trying to be more sensitive and supportive, we seem to have over-steered to correct a problem and have almost wrecked on the other side of the road. They feel entitled, and we have agreed! No one meant for it to happen... it just happened.

The concept of entitlement can best be understood by substituting an easily recognized word... spoiled! To say that they are synonymous though is an over simplification. They are both in the same ball park, but entitlement is a dynamic that grows out of a misalliance between parents and children as the child is growing up. Somehow, parents tend to communicate, and the child seems to hear, that the special love parents have for them allows or entitles them to special privileges, or to believe they are exceptions to the rule. This can lead to a condition called narcissism, the attitude that a person not only feels special (which they are), but feels extra special (which they are not)!

If this dynamic begins early on in a child's life and continues into young adulthood, the stage is set for young adults to have expectations of their parents and for themselves that are totally unrealistic. This dynamic can be so ingrained that it is very difficult to change, even if the young adults recognizes it and want to change it for themselves.

As previously stated, we baby boomers sometimes (many times) are overly concerned about what our children will think about us for doing no other than being responsible parents. And we are worried about what they might do with their lives if we do not 'help' and comply with their wishes. When I became a parent, and later a step-parent, I too seemed to become codependent on our children. I have to work at being autonomous and not give up my ability to self-govern. Yes, I must confess, I am a recovering co-deparent!

To summarize this sociological reason, when we as baby boomers were growing up, the prevailing mantra was, 'children are to be seen and not heard.' However, as young adults and young parents influenced by a more sensitive environment, we realized that children (of all ages) indeed needed to be seen and heard! What seems to have happened was that somewhere in listening to our children, we 'lost our own voice' and are now trying to find it once again.

Secondly, besides the era in which baby boomers grew up, there is another reason we have this crisis in autonomy and codependency. Many times we have an under-developed sense of self and emotional security. Where the first factor is more sociological, this dynamic is more psychological. The first reason is interpersonal, the second is intrapersonal.

Developmental psychologists tell us that in the first two/three years of life, a process goes on between a child and his/her primary caregiver that tends to set the tone for whether or not we self-govern throughout life, barring significant intervention. Having gotten this far, we need to go on an inward journey and look at the extremely important but hidden dynamic that takes place within each of us as individuals.

Just as there is an outward and observable physical maturation process from birth to age three, there is an inward and much less observable maturation process that takes place inside each of us from birth to age three. We call this process the development of a sense of self; a recognition of our unique personhood, a discovery that we are a person in our own right, separate from our parents and the rest of the world.

On occasion, I teach a class at our local community college on childhood development. At the beginning of each semester I ask the students at what age they think we become a person, or developmentally have a solid sense of self? Consistently, I get answers ranging from early teens to young adult. In fact, this process begins at birth, or genetically, before birth, and is well established by age 3+. This is a difficult concept for students and for many adults to understand.

So, what follows is a brief (very brief) description of this inward process which, if understood, can help explain to a large extent our lack of autonomy and the codependent dynamics that tend to make it so difficult for us to parent our problematic young adults. It will also help us understand why our young adults have so much trouble accepting our parenting and being responsible individuals.

From those who have studied early childhood development, it appears that when an infant is born, and for several months after, the infant identifies with the mother and has no sense that he is a person in his own right. It is believed that the infant feels he and his mother are one person because all his needs for survival are continuing to be met. Then gradually, the infant becomes a young child and starts to see that he and his mother are two different beings. When the mother leaves the room, the child becomes upset since he has also come to see he is dependent on the mother for his life (or at least his basic needs). With reassurance from the mother, the child, now crawling and later walking, can come and go with security. Even though he is still dependent on his mother for some basic needs, he does not die if he is not constantly in the presence of his mother or primary caregiver. He starts to see that he can meet many of his own needs. At the same time, the mother also sees the infant as a separate individual who slowly but surely becomes capable of meeting some of his own needs. By this point in his development, the toddler, around age two, is determined to think for himself and even insists on "doing it by myself". He is striving for the first time to be autonomous and wants his mother to give him the freedom to do so...mistakes and all. Thus, at around age three (if both mother and child survived age two), the toddler can come and go on his own, meet many of his own needs, and both he and the less anxious mother can relate as two separate individuals. The Separation-Individuation (S-I) process is well underway.*

For us as individuals it is our own successful S-I process from our parents that leads to a secure sense of self and also leads us to become a secure self-governing parent who is not as codependent on his/her young adult. We can be more responsible to our grown children and our grown children can be more responsible for themselves. On the other hand, if this S-I process is not as successful, the stage is set for being less prepared to parent young adults who have difficulty accepting responsibilities for themselves.

It is more difficult for us to say no, set limits, etc., and to let our young adults live their own lives…mistakes and all.

When we agree with our young adults that they are extra special folks who are entitled to whatever they want, and we are not secure enough to set limits with them for fear of what they will think of us or will do to themselves, we stand a good chance of depending on them for our security and happiness. When they have problems not being able to help themselves, much less us, our fear - lack of autonomy - enables them to continue to live irresponsible lifestyles resulting in unhappiness for all. Barring some kind of positive change in this process, these issues can continue to be active and detrimental to us, to our young adult relationship, and to others who may be involved.

It is my hope that the remainder of this book will reinforce our own sense of personhood as individuals and as parents; help us be more autonomous and less codependent; and take better care of ourselves as we try to help our problematic young adults.

The Reader's Page

Chapter 3

Problematic Issues of Young Adults

Let's now look at some problem issues that are confronting many of us parents of young adults and the context in which they present themselves. Not in any particular order of importance, for that varies with each of us, I'll simply begin with financial concerns and their implications.

Financial Problems

As parents, we work hard every day, hold down a responsible job, and earn a salary. We pay bills, try to save for retirement (which for some of us baby boomers is only a few years away), and hopefully enjoy ourselves on occasion. Often times, our problematic young adult either does not hold down a job or if he/she does, fails to spend their money responsibly. Instead, they incur bills they do not pay, and ask us for money to pay them. Even if there is not a direct request to pay or help pay their bills, our awareness of their situation, many times results in our self-imposed feeling of obligation to bail them out.

Now, if this is a one time or occasional situation, that is one thing. But if it has become a way of life, that's a different situation. Our need to 'help' them, if this is a pattern of life, is not help at all, it is a stepping stone 'enabling' them to continue to have problems with their finances. Much like when they were young children and wanted to eat cookies right before a meal and we said no, or only one, because it would ruin their appetite. We knew that if we let them have all the sweets they wanted, we would have to accept part of the responsibility for them not wanting their veggies. In like manner, if we continue to pay for the things the young adults have the appetite for but do not pay for, we must realize that we are not helping, but hurting the ones we love.

Let's look specifically at some generic examples of how this financial issue manifests itself and its implications for parenting.

Example one: Our young adult either does not want to hold down a job or works at a job which does not provide medical or dental benefits. We have encouraged her to do so, many times, but she wants the freedom, or less responsibility that this job provides. She does not choose to face the implications that could occur with a medical or dental crisis. We become aware of her need for either a crown or dental implant. Now, if this were a back tooth, we'd think 'let her have it pulled and that's that.' But if it's a front tooth! To make things yet more complicated, she does not want a bridge because it would mean grinding down each tooth, so she wants an implant which will cost several thousand dollars!

The question at this point for us is how do we handle the situation? What do we say to our beautiful, but financially irresponsible young adult? Do we say, "You made your bed, now you'll have to lie in it. I warned you this might happen." Do we let her have the tooth pulled and be snaggle-toothed for the rest of her life (or for now)? Just what? Or, does her emotional pressure on us or our own self-imposed expectations cause us to go to the bank, borrow the money, and once again pay her out of the situation?

I shudder to think what might happen if a serious and/or chronic medical condition should occur and there is no insurance. The financial implications to us could be catastrophic! It is possible that we could lose everything if we do not have a handle on the codependent dynamics in relationships with our young adults.

Example two: Our young adult finally got himself a job and is earning some money, but his taste is more expensive than his salary can afford. He buys a brand new thirty-thousand dollar pick-up truck. The payments are $500.00 per month and his budgeting skills are not such that he can make the payments. He asks us to help him on a regular basis to make the monthly payments. We don't want him to let the truck have to be repossessed because it will be a black mark on his credit rating, and with no vehicle, he has no transportation to get to work. So, we help him with the monthly payments even though it is a strain on our own budget! Then, we happen by his apartment one weekend and see in his back yard a fully equipped fishing boat and trailer which has to have cost several thousand dollars! He proudly announces that it is his (on monthly payments) and that he and his buddies plan to do some serious fishing.

What do we do? Angry? You bet! We tell him that we have 'had it' and that he is now on his own with both his truck and boat payments! Later, we begin to worry about him and what this will do to our relationship with him. The proverbial second guess, self imposed guilt routine. Well! What is one to do?

Example three: Our young adult insists on moving out into her own apartment but isn't sure how she can afford it by herself. So, she seeks a roommate to share the rent and expenses with her. She and her roommate do not get along, roomie leaves, and our young adult gets stuck with all the rent herself. For the second or third time, when we come home from a trip and open the garage door, we see her 'stuff' back home! We go inside, she has taken up residence in her old room again, unwashed dishes are in the sink, dirty clothes and wet towels are on the bathroom floor. She is fast asleep on the living room sofa. (Oh yes, it's 2:00 in the afternoon!) Parents' blood pressure goes through the roof, we wake her up and exchange harsh words. She, crying, gets a few of her belongings, says since she is not welcome there, she will leave, and out the door she goes! As we are unloading the car, we start worrying about where she'll go, what she'll do, and feel totally confused, guilty, and miserable. What to do?

Example four: Our young adult is struggling, one job after another. He approaches us about an idea for a financial undertaking that he is sure will work for him, but needs us to co-sign with him to borrow money to get started on his project. Against our better judgment, we co-sign the loan. Yep, just what we thought, his project is not working out, he abandons the efforts and the bank now looks to us to pay them back. Our young adult does not seem overly concerned about this and we are again frustrated, unhappy and completely at a loss as to how to handle the situation. None-the-less, we have to come up with the money (if we can – mortgage the house?) to pay off the loan.

Example five: Our young adult, after several years of searching as to what to do, announces he is now ready to settle down, go to college, and make something of himself. We are excited about this prospect and happy for him and ourselves as well. We have been hoping and praying that he would "find himself" and do something positive with his life. Now, of all things, he is ready to go to college! Our assumption is that he will start at the local community college, keep his expenses and costs down for at least the first two years to see if this is truly what he wants to do, then transfer to a four-year college to finish up. When he meets with us to discuss his plans and how we could possibly assist him, he excitedly announces he wants to go to a four-year school, rent an apartment (not live in a dorm), and get serious about his studies. When we suggest some alternative thoughts about this, he is either angry, upset and irritated, or disappointed in our ideas and says, "Just forget it!" Wanting to support him, we make financial arrangements, contact him and say, "Work out the details, and you'll be off to college." Toward the end of the first quarter, it is evident that he is not going to pass three out of four classes. When we talk with him about this, he says that it was his roommates who caused the problem but not to worry, they are moving out, and he will have the apartment all to himself next semester. Right! With us to foot the whole rent for him! When we suggest a dorm room, he says it could never work out…too much going on there for quality study time! What to do?

Relationship Problems

Secondly, besides financial concerns, relationship concerns can cause a parent of a young adult to be extremely stressed.

When our child is younger and problems arise as to his/her choice of friends, we seem to have more influence, and even some control in their relationships, especially if they are potentially unhealthy ones. However, in parenting young adults and their choices of friends and significant others, we are not in the same position and rightly so. With younger children, we are in some sense still teaching them how to choose healthy relationships and are quite involved in their social lives. Not so in parenting young adults and their choice of relationships and friendships. It is no longer in our job description to be as involved in the process. In fact, in most cases our young adults are not asking us for our help with these choices. And in other cases they definitely do not want our input, especially if the relationships are unhealthy.

Let's now look at some examples of unhealthy relationships in which, if we are not careful, we might be even more unhappy than our young adult.

Example one: We find out that our 19 year old daughter is dating a 26 year old man who is divorced, has three younger children, is "in between jobs" and is thinking about moving into the apartment that we are helping her pay the rent on. Oh, by the way, she tells us that his ex is an extremely aggressive woman who is making threatening comments to her. Our daughter also tells us that she thinks she is in love with him, he makes her feel so special, and she also loves his children even though his six year old daughter is having "just a little trouble adjusting to her". But she feels in time that it will all work out, especially if they were to get married and become "one big happy family".

When we begin to talk with her about some of the possible problematic issues, she becomes defensive, and says we are not giving her boyfriend a chance, and if that's the way we are going to be, she will just not come around. Besides, he has already told her if his ex continues to bother or threaten her, she can call 911 and the police will put a stop to it.

Example two: We are concerned and stressed over our son's plans to marry a young woman whom he has been dating for several years. He believes that marriage would cement their relationship. On a number of occasions she has "stepped-out" on him and has also broken up with him to date other men. More than one time our son has been so despondent that his feelings turned into a serious depression. We have spent time with him during these periods and have tried to support his decision. He is a thirty-year old man with a responsible job and is buying his own home. However, when we have tried to discuss the serious problems in his relationship to this woman, he is not receptive and we can see that it might damage our relationship to him if we continue to discourage him. His response to us is that we don't really know her, and he believes she is ready to settle down. She has also told him that he is now her one and only. (Oh yes, we inadvertently became aware only yesterday that her car was seen at a motel in a nearby town!) What's a parent to do with a son who is in an addictive/codependent relationship?

Or, what is a parent to do if we are the parent of this troubled young woman?

It is obvious that examples having to do with unhealthy relationships in which our problematic young adults can be involved are many and complicated. These relationships can run the gamut, all of which can leave us as parents even unhappier than our unhappy troubled young adults if we cannot find ways to take care of ourselves.

Alcohol and Drug Problems

The problems with alcohol and drug dependency are one of, if not the most critical problems in which a troubled young adult can be involved. They are problems that have the potential of destroying everyone who is associated with them – us as parents, as well as our participating young adult.

I don't believe one could imagine any area of our lives that is not affected by this horrific problem. Of all the issues we can come up against, this well might be the toughest. Especially is this so because this particular problem involves a biochemical addictive process from which it is difficult to recover. Matter of fact, those in the field of alcohol and drug treatment speak of being in recovery, not of being recovered! Also, this problem often involves legal issues that can have consequences even when the participant is in recovery. 'Helpless' only scratches the surface of what a parent feels when their precious young adult is caught in the grip of drugs. To see a son or daughter addicted to alcohol or drugs and know the serious, even life threatening consequences in their lives creates a black hole in our lives. Too many times we realize there is little we can do for them until they alone decide to ask for, participate in, and take responsibility for their own recovery.

With these and other serious problems like them, we ask, "How is it even possible to be happy as a parent in such situations?" Well, the answer is, we cannot! That is, we can't be as happy as we could be if the situation were different. However, we are still valued persons in our own right. We may have a spouse whom we love and who loves us, other responsible children who need us, and/or friends and relationships who deserve our shared efforts in maintaining those relationships. Life goes on despite the problems affecting us! Yes, I know. "But…but, what in the world does one do?"

Other Problematic Issues

Since it is not possible or feasible for me to look at all the problems in which our young adults can be involved, I must depend on you, the reader, to use the Reader's Page to list the unique concerns you have for your own situation. Then, later when we are addressing ways to think about and work with the problems, in a personalized way, you can apply these concepts to you and your young adult.

Now, let's move on to those concepts that hopefully will be of help to us as we apply them in our lives and to the lives of our troubled young adults.

Footnote: The above problematic issues are generic and do not reflect the experiences of any individual or family other than the Martins'.

The Reader's Page

Chapter 4

<u>Healthy Coping Concepts</u>

In the earlier days of the development of psychology and the behavioral sciences, a concept was discovered that has proven over and over again to be of great help in dealing with and coping with many of life's problems. The basic premise to this coping concept is, "An idea can make you sick and an idea can make you well." This dynamic has now been used very effectively in the therapeutic and counseling fields for more than a hundred years. When a person presents with a problem they have not been able to resolve, the counselor can, along with that person, explore other ways to look at the situation that could provide some different answers and/or different results.

In similar fashion I am suggesting that we consider another way of looking at trying to help our problematic young adults while simultaneously helping ourselves. It is essential that we take as much care of ourselves as we try to take care of our irresponsible young adults. In doing so, we make the paradigm shift of starting with ourselves and then moving on to the needs of our young adult.

I have called these ideas: Healthy Coping Concepts. And, in many ways these concepts make up the heart of the book. They at least take up most of the pages in it.

The format I have chosen to use to talk about these Healthy Coping Concepts is one modeled after the developmental approach used by Erik Erikson in his discussion of the developmental task begun at age one and continued throughout life.* This is not a judgmental set of guidelines meant to make us feel bad as parents when we are less than successful but rather the sharing of ideas to help us use good judgment in self-care and parenting. These coping concepts and their application in our lives will help us grow in our ability to self-govern (autonomy) and decrease our unhealthy dependence (codependence) on our young adults. Also, it is my hope that we will have a healthier relationship with our young adults as well as in some extreme cases save our emotional lives.

Control of Self vs. Control of Young Adults

In coping with these issues we would do well to consider the concept of being in charge/control of our own lives and not in trying to be in control of our young adult's life. In my experience, controlling oneself in relation to one's young adults is a full time job.

It is likely more of an illusion than a reality to think that we have the power or influence to control any other person, especially an irresponsible young adult or our grown children. Attempting this tact could also potentially present ethical issues.

I understand, however, that driven by the seriousness of the problems our young adults are experiencing, and by our wanting so much to "help", we sometimes resort to efforts to control not only their irresponsible behavior, but even their way of thinking that leads to such behavior. With this understanding in mind, let's address the advisability and effectiveness of trying to do so.

One emotional mechanism we use to exert control is guilt. Such statements as the following reflect this: (Any of these sound familiar?) "If you loved us, you would not ..."or, "Are you just trying to hurt us?" or, "You're killing us!" The ineffectiveness of this approach is that one of the young adult's problems is lack of a sense of empathy to feel what we are feeling and the inability to clearly see how what they do effects us. (After all, "...it's their life!") Many of them have an underdeveloped conscience and do not feel guilt as we do.

It seems that because of our lack of autonomy and our codependency on them, we find ourselves in a situation where the tail is wagging the dog. Since this "control/being in charge of" approach does not work well, especially over the long-haul, I'm suggesting we emphasize controlling ourselves, managing better our lives in relationship to the problems of our young adults.

Symbolically speaking, we must spend more energy driving our own cars and letting our young adults drive theirs! And if we find ourselves riding in their car with them and they are driving dangerously, we must stop trying to tell them how to drive (that ended at age 16 or 17), and instead control our own lives by asking them to stop and let us get out. Hopefully they will respond positively to our self-care and slow their dangerous actions down, thus, taking better care of themselves in the process.

A good rule of thumb that I try to operate by is to have a minimum of 51% of the say-so in my own life. That's at least a simple majority of the control. If we can have and maintain that, we can operate in healthier ways in relation to our out-of-control young adult.

Assertive vs. Passive or Aggressive

There are evidently a number of ways to achieve having the primary say-so in our own lives. One of these is to be more assertive in relationship to the young adult who is having serious problems. Assertiveness means letting our child know, in an appropriate way, what we will and will not do, as opposed to trying to tell or get them to do or not do something. This latter approach would be more of an aggressive approach which usually is not received well by our young adult and problems are sometimes made even worse. In reality, parents cannot make their young adult do or not do something. If we do that, we revert back to trying to control them with all its implications.

On the other hand, if we take a passive approach (not asserting our feelings and thoughts), this could be seen as agreeing with some irresponsible decision and of course, this is not the better approach either. Also, if we take a passive approach, we begin to resent what is happening and eventually explode in an aggressive outburst which can seriously damage our relationship. We too, then, would be partly responsible for the problem(s) this approach caused. Why? Because we ourselves would be out of control! Remember, our goal is control of self, not control of others.

Here is what I call the "I-need-money-for-gas-in-the-car-to-keep-my-job" example. The story line is that after not having a job for months, finally our young adult gets a job, and late on

Sunday night informs us that they need money to put gas in their car to get to work Monday morning. Now, we have been relieved that they indeed have a job and are doing better in paying their own bills. However, we are also aware that to give cash to put gas in their car is not the best or wisest thing to do. Why? Because in the past, the money was not used solely for gas and the gas money request happened all over again in a day or two.

So, instead of agreeing to give gas money and risking a confrontation when the request comes again, we let our young adult know what we will do and that is, "Let's go down to the gas station and I'll pay for the gas in your car and I can fill up, too."

If our young adult agrees, then there is no problem. If they say they don't feel like going out, we say, "Then we can meet in the morning and fill our tanks up together before work." If they say okay, again no problem. If they say, "I don't have to get up as early as you, just give me the gas money," then it is a situation where we must work on controlling ourselves and not trying to control them. We assertively say again what we will or will not do. That is, we will be glad to fill their tank tonight or in the morning but we will not give them the cash. It's then up to them to accept or refuse our offer.

Perfect vs. Good Enough Parent

Have you ever said, "I know I'm not perfect but...". I contend there is no but! We are not perfect! Ok, then what? Then we work on being "good enough" parents.

When one first hears the concept of a good enough parent, most people think of a mediocre parent. Not so. The good enough parent is in fact preferable to the "perfect parent" in many ways. Not the least of which is in parenting young adults with serious problems.

A brief history lesson at this point might be in order. In the mid- 1900's a man by the name of D.W. Winnicott, first coined the term "good enough parent" as he observed how mothers parented their infants. As he watched mothers parent their children, he divided them into three categories. The perfect parent, the negligent parent, and the good enough parent. The perfect parent did too much for their infants, not allowing them to learn how to do for themselves. The negligent parent did not do enough for their infants in helping them learn and thus left a sense of hopelessness in them. The good enough parent, on the other hand, seemed to have the correct balance of participation in the child's life allowing them the opportunity to learn how to do for themselves and directly intervened only when needed; as of course one would do when the situation demanded it. *

Winnicott reported being able to follow some of these infants and their parents into adulthood and found that the good enough parent and their good enough young adults fared far better in most cases than did the children raised by the negligent or "perfect parent."

I'm assuming that any parent of a young adult reading these words, more than likely does not fall into the negligent parent category but instead struggles with how to best participate in the life and problems of their young adult. Or, one who is trying to be the best parent they know how to be. Right? Of course, that's right! So, how does a good enough parent participate in the problems, poor decision making, and otherwise irresponsible choices of young adults? Basically, the less we can do for the young adult and the more the young adult can do for himself, the more preferable it is. We must recognize that we do not have all the answers and also recognize our young adult must come to grips with their own life. For if we do everything, or most everything, for them, try to be the "perfect parent", we are not helping them nearly as much as we might think. Just as in Winnicott's observation, our indulgence limits the young adult in learning how to do for themselves. It also drains more time and energy than we can healthfully handle, leaving us depleted and our young adult ignorant of many of the life skills they need for success.

Good, better, or best? The best way is just doing the best you can, and for me, that's good enough. What say you?

Footnote: I cannot leave this concept without one additional word. Not only is the "perfect parent" not the preferable parenting position to take, especially with problematic young adults, but it is one that can be of least help to our young adults. Why? Because with all their problems and basic human imperfections, they have little or no chance to do it the "perfect way" like their "perfect parent." In essence, they fail before they even get started. And, of course, the "perfect parent" then feels they have failed too, with all its negative implications.

Responsible To vs. Responsible For

I believe that most parents want to be responsible parents. However, by definition it is easy to feel responsible for our problematic young adult but when that happens, it is less likely that our young adults will feel responsible for themselves.

It is true that when our children are young, we are indeed responsible for them and their actions. However, when we are referring to young adults, we are not responsible for them or their actions at any level: personally, socially, legally, spiritually, financially, etc. They are responsible for themselves and we are responsible to them, but only responsible for ourselves. This is not a play on words but a statement of a very important concept in parenting young adults. A concept that if not understood and applied can make things even more difficult for us as parents and not at all helpful for the irresponsible young adult.

It is easier to understand the above concept when applied to situations our young adults may face. For example, if they break the law (and are 18 years old or older), we cannot go to court for them, regardless of how much they might want us to. Some parents would rather take the punishment themselves, but the law does not permit it. Obviously, there are a number of similar issues when, despite the irresponsible young adult's wish for the parents to be responsible for them and the parent's desire to be such, it is just not possible.

There are many instances and many issues where parents are tempted to and do take responsibility for the irresponsibility of their young adults. One such area is financial obligations the young adult is not living up to. But by paying their own bills, they have made a step toward financial responsibility. We therein have infused the goal of our self-care, maintained our parental obligation to them, and placed the onus of responsibility for themselves squarely on their shoulders.

Punishment vs. Natural or Logical Consequences

A young adult does not need to be punished for their irresponsibility, but does need to be allowed to experience the logical consequences of such; just as we would experience if we were not responsible for our own obligations.

Most of us find it extremely difficult to allow our young adult to experience the natural or logical consequences of their poor choices. We try to "help" them out so they will feel better or won't be upset. This of course usually is not help to them or to ourselves in the long-run because it enables them to avoid the negative consequences of irresponsible choices.

And, another potential negative consequence of our "help" is that it often backfires on us. When our invested time, energy, caring, love, and financial support do not produce the desired results (progress towards them becoming more responsible), we become increasingly frustrated and upset and react with punishment and/or anger, further exacerbating the already unhealthy parent/child relationship.

Grief vs. Anger/Guilt

When our young adults do not act responsibly, some of our first feelings are worry and concern, soon followed by increasing anger and guilt; anger at our young adults for being the way they are and guilt for our anger towards them. Our fear is of having "failed" to be good parents and possibly "causing" them to be the way they are by something(s) we have or have not done.

The energy and efforts we use in being angry and guilty are of very little help to all parties concerned and is potentially harmful to our relationship with our young adult.

Anger is frequently a cover emotion and very seldom "rides alone."* Other emotions such as hurt, embarrassment and grief lurk beneath the feeling of anger. It is these deeper and hidden feelings that most of us have, but may not be aware of or if aware, are not sure how to handle in a constructive way.

Once we get in touch with our anger and sadness/grief, we come to see that we are not as angry over problems and irresponsible decisions as we are extremely sad and need to grieve the situation we find ourselves in.

As to the feeling of guilt, we can begin by saying that indeed we have done some things poorly in parenting our young children as well as young adult children. As pointed out earlier, we are not perfect parents and are willing to admit in a healthy way we have some responsibility for some of the problematic issues our young adults struggle with. However, as John Bradshaw points out, many of us are experiencing "toxic guilt" that is neither healthy nor helpful.* To feel guilt over our mistakes is appropriate but to feel guilty over our young adult's mistakes is to be experiencing unhealthy (toxic) guilt.

Many of us, probably most of us, find it very difficult to accept the sad fact that sometimes there is little we can do or say to help our young adult make more responsible decisions.

However, that is exactly what is needed. We need to be in touch with our grief and experience our sad feelings just as we do with other areas in our lives where grief is appropriate.

Until we grieve, we will continue to be stuck between anger and guilt. When we let ourselves feel sadness and experience the grief, we can begin the process of recovery. As Elizabeth Kubler Ross shared with us years ago in her work on *Death and Dying*, grief has stages. As we work through these stages we begin to get unstuck, begin to recover, and begin to heal from our sadness.** With this healing comes the hope that we will not continue to be angry at them for their irresponsibility but rather love them even though sadly, sometimes we cannot help them.

Attitude vs. Action

A veterinarian friend of mine once shared with me that in vet school one of his professors was fond of saying to his students when presented with a problem of some sort, "Don't just do something, stand there!" And, in similar fashion I encourage those of us as parents of young adults with serious problems to concentrate more on our own attitude than on our actions.

Applying what we have discussed so far will help us develop an attitude(s) that will help us and many times help our young adults more than our actions will or could.

There are a number of ways that we can apply this concept. The idea of possibly being as unhappy as our young adult really stands out in my mind.

If our attitude is one of having to be miserable most of the time to be a good parent, this will push us to constantly be trying to do things that "fix" our young adult's problems, placing our emphasis on actions. If our attitude is one of being responsible for ourselves and to our young adults, we will not feel so guilty over being able to enjoy our lives and our actions will reflect such.

In addition and even more importantly, remembering if indeed an attitude can make us sick or an attitude can make us well, and if we conceptualize our role as a parent to be living our young adult's life, then we must be prepared for a hard row to hoe. If our attitude is one of loving our young adult, being responsible for ourselves and to them, doing the best we can to help out when they do their part, trying not to feel guilty for trying to be happy ourselves, then and only then can we avoid actions that hurt the situation and the relationship. Keep in mind the goal is not allowing ourselves to become as unhappy as they are.

Judgmental vs. Good Judgment

Speaking from experience, I have not found it to be helpful when others have been judgmental of me when I have made poor choices or shown less than good decision making abilities. But I have usually responded in a positive, less defensive way when encouraged to use better judgment about my decisions and actions. What about you? What about your young adult?

Condemning our young adult for their problems is like offering a drowning person a glass of water. Recommending some other/better ways to solve their problems, i.e., suggesting the use of good judgment and then allowing them the choice to do their own decision making with its natural/logical consequences is a far more helpful and healthy way to relate.

Please don't misunderstand, or better yet, please let me not miscommunicate this very important concept. I am not saying we don't need to be firm in our convictions as to the use of good judgment and in assertively communicating these, but we do very little if any good by making our young adults feel worse than they already do (and many, in fact, do feel like failures).

The key concept in this section is applicable in tandem. When we make the very best decisions we are capable of in what we feel is the best interest of our children, given the time and circumstance, we must not be condemning nor judgmental of ourselves if they fail to produce the desired outcome. For, as I have stressed several times before, if you are reading this book, I'm relatively certain you are doing, and have done, the best you can with a complicated and complex situation. We cannot judge our success as parents by what our young adults do with their choices in life, only by what we do with the choices we make for own lives.

Consistency vs. Inconsistency

The concept of consistency for helping us and our young adults may seem quite obvious, and in fact, it is. However, like many obvious things we can overlook their importance.

In applying any of the concepts previously addressed, or those to come, it is extremely important that once we are convinced this is what we need and possibly what our young adult needs, then doing what we say and saying what we do will provide a stability to our lives and situation. In like manner, to be inconsistent can cause more instability than we already have.

For example, if we tell our young adult that we are no longer going to pay his cell phone bill, especially since it is $200-$300.00 per month, then we do as we have said and not pay it. Allow our young adult to experience the natural consequences, either positive or negative, as a way to learn from his mistakes or benefit from paying the bill himself. If we say we are not going to pay their car payment, rent, etc., from then on, it is important to do just that. If we aren't consistent, neither they nor we can count on what we say.

There may be exceptions to what we are saying here, but they need to be few, few, few if we are to have peace and stability in our lives.

Food/Shelter/Clothing vs. Money/Money/Money

Depending on the extent of the financial problems our young adult experiences, especially his/her difficulty in being financially responsible, this concept may apply less or more. Most of us, however, can relate to the situation of having given our young adult money to buy food, or clothes, or to pay their rent, only to find the money was spent not for these necessities but for various luxuries, so to speak. And, this may have happened over and over until we became upset, frustrated and possibly out of money ourselves.

In trying to see to it that our young adult is not starving, give them food, not money! See to it that they have adequate clothing, not money! Try to provide them with at least temporary shelter if needed, not money! In this way our worries over these basic needs will be addressed without our having to worry about whether they have "blown" the money or not.

It is extremely important in these situations not to give money. To do so is further enabling their financial irresponsibility and that is not helping them.

I am convinced that to offer only material possessions is to offer only a temporary solution to their problems and it is not fulfilling to us as parents. However, to offer who we are to them, or to try to, is to offer our concern, our experience, our essence, and our availability. When we do this, whether received or not, we know we have given all we really could that would have any lasting positive effects for us and for them.

One way to apply this concept is anytime we are asked directly or indirectly to give, loan or let borrow, our money, our car, our signature on a loan, our clothes, etc., we ask our young adult to spend time letting us know the details of their needs and giving us an opportunity to let them know our thoughts and feelings about their situation. Be sure that this is not a lecture session nor an attempt at trying to make our young adult see things our way. What we are hoping for is that our young adult will get to know us a little better and we will get to know them better also.

There may or may not be an exchange of our stuff; this is not the main objective to try to accomplish.

Special vs. Extra Special

As I pointed out earlier, many of our young adults feel they are not only special (which we all are) but for various inward and outward reasons they feel that they are extra special (which they, nor we, are). With this entitlement attitude, a number of unrealistic expectations exists. It almost comes across as 'I deserve this or that', especially in relationship to us as their parents.

Now, if we too buy into this extra special feeling, we will collude with our young adult, setting us all up for more heartache, misunderstanding and miscommunication. But, if we conceptualize each person as a unique, special individual who does need love and support, then we bring clarity to our relationship.

Entitlement is not the healthy expectation. The hope and expectation is that our basic needs will be met as small children by our parents and increasingly by ourselves as we mature. The goal is not to meet these needs for our young adults; we meet these needs for ourselves. The goal is to appropriately expect our young adults to do for themselves as we assist them in a secondary, not primary way.

We certainly get the cart before the horse when either our young adults or we expect that we should do for our children what they can do for themselves. Assisting them when we can as they take the lead in their lives is a much better approach for all concerned.

Relationship vs. Teaching

I'm not sure exactly why it is (I have a few ideas though) that young adults don't seem to be able to learn from the experiences of their parents. Young adults, including ourselves when we were their age, seem to have to learn mainly from their own experiences. Why then do we continue to try to teach at the cost of our relationship with them?

Certainly, we have the responsibility and privilege to teach our younger children and teens as they are growing up. There comes a point, sooner for troubled children and young adults, when we seem to have very little influence but continue to try to teach, teach, teach. This leads to frustration for us and begins to negatively impact our relationship. They resist, resist, resist and the relationship is damaged.

There are many implications to this damaging dynamic. One of the most serious is that when we could assist our young adults in a healthy way, we are unable to because of the damaged relationship. We end up losing emotional and sometimes physical contact because we were so determined or felt compelled to try to teach them.

The decision is ours. Will we continue to try to teach our troubled young adult at the expense of the relationship, or will we focus on the relationship with the hope that our young adult will learn form their own experience? It's evident where I stand at this point. What about you?

Loving Up Close vs. Loving From a Distance

It is important for us to realize that if our relationship with our young adult is injured or strained, all is not lost. Hope lies in the concept of loving at a distance if we are unable to love up close.

When, for whatever reason, it is not possible to give and receive up close love, we need to realize that love and concern is not dependent on emotional and physical closeness. Our love continues even though we might be angry, hurt, frustrated, or discouraged and feel hopeless to reach them. It continues even though our young adult might not believe that we love them since we are not enabling them in their poor decisions.

Realizing that love counts up close or from a distance can help us cope and can be extremely comforting. It is still very relevant even when it is at a distance. Sad, yes, but still meaningful.

Setting Limits vs. Limitless

Where love can be seen as limitless, "No matter what, I still love you," many other aspects of our relationship need to have some healthy limits. I question if it is love for them or love of ourselves if there are no limits to what we are willing to do. If we are not able to set limits, I question if we are not overly concerned, even codependent on them for our happiness. We can't say no because we run the risk of making them unhappy and if they're unhappy, so are we.

In setting limits remember the thesis of this book: If we are not careful we might not be any happier than our unhappiest child. We do not want to be unhappier than one has to be from life in general, so it is important to work on setting limits.

Since our problematic young adults have trouble setting limits and this causes serious problems, we need to come to believe that it is better for all concerned if limits are set and kept. Not to do so is to unintentionally join with them and their poor decisions and the consequences of such. Not to set limits would be like giving them a signed blank check to our savings account! (Uh-huh! Thought that would wake you up if this is making you sleepy or if it seems too much to have to do and you are wondering if it's all worth it.)

Yes. It is all worth it if we want the best for ourselves and the best we can offer them. As we know in these tough situations, the best sometimes means barely getting by, but the other options are not at all good. Limits are our friend and our young adult's friend. To allow or to participate in a limitless relationship is to hurt those who, for various reasons, cannot set their own limits. Their appetite/wants feel so great to them and they make so many poor choices about wanting these that they get into a downward spiral which they cannot pull out of. At least by setting limits on what we will and will not do, we can help them not spiral downward any deeper than they could go on their own.

Just Say No vs. Just Say Yes

Speaking of setting limits, one of the most difficult things for most parents to do in dealing with the requests of our problematic young adults is to just say, "NO!" It is also one of the most healthy and responsible things we can do for them and do to take care of ourselves.

Possibly the main reason it is so important to be able to say no to our young adults is that it is one of the things they have trouble doing. You say, "What?" Let me clarify this point by saying they have the most trouble saying no to their appetite for their wants and needs. (Of course, we know all too well that they are much better at saying no to us and to our needs and wants.) If they cannot say no, and we do not say no, one can see the problems this can cause for us all.

Many of our heartaches can be prevented if we can come to believe that saying no is the best thing we can do. Or, if we have already said yes, then we must move toward modifying our position. Saying no can help move toward the best solution and help salvage what we can of money, time, our mental and physical energy, etc.

Remember, the more we work toward being autonomous parents and less codependent on our young adults, the more we can assertively say no when they seem to be unable to. In this way we are able to express our care for them since we are in control of our decisions and are choosing not to enable them and their poor choices. Our young adults are less likely to proceed toward more serious problems, debts, and whatever, if we refuse to bankroll their efforts.

Autocratic vs. Democratic

It is so easy to fall into the trap of trying to tell our young adults how to live their lives, especially since they are doing such a poor job of it by all standards. We know the challenges of trying to take care of ourselves while trying to parent our young adults but, and I mean but, without any formal authority to do such. This is one of the main reasons the autocratic approach no longer works. We have no teeth behind what we say. I don't believe in the autocratic father or mother who always knows the best approach when parenting, but that is more of a personal opinion than fact. I feel it simply will not work. Unless our young adult is willing to let us tell them what to do and how to live their life, we will continue to be unhappy and frustrated by trying to make them be responsible for themselves and their actions.

In a democratic approach of relating to our young adults, each represents himself, has authority over himself and is responsible for himself, - one person, one vote. One's life is in his or her own hands and it is the young adult who decides what type of life that will be, not us as their parents.

I once heard a story about an older man who was known throughout his community to be very wise. A young boy decided to try and trick this older gentleman and prove him to be not as wise as others said. So, the boy caught a bird, held it behind his back out of sight of the man and asked him if the bird was alive or dead. The boy's thinking was that if the man said the bird was dead he would release the bird to fly away, and if the man said the bird was alive, he would squeeze it to death. In either case he would prove the older gentleman wrong. After thinking for a few minutes, the man replied "The answer to the question is in your own hands!"

We have our hands full just trying to live our own lives , let alone trying to live or be in charge of our young adult's lives, no matter how problematic and needy they might be. It's not that we always know best; we can only try to do our best.

<u>Empathy vs. Sympathy</u>

As loving parents, our hearts go out in the deepest way toward our young adults as they struggle to live their lives. We connect with the pain and frustration they go through and hurt for them even when they bring much of this on themselves. So, in large part, our unhappiness is due to their unhappiness.

In order to keep from worrying ourselves into an early grave and be respectful of what our young adults are feeling and experiencing, we must recognize that we are not living their lives for them or with them. They are separate individuals from us with ways of thinking and feeling that are different from and independent of ours. In exercising self-care, our pain is more indirect, secondary from their more primary, direct pain. We feel sorry for them (sympathy) and feel with them (empathy) but we are not them. I believe we do a disservice to our young adults and to ourselves if we feel sorry for their pain to the extent that we cannot separate their pain from ours. We need to recognize that we are not them...we feel for them, but we can be happy (as much as possible) despite their choices and the ensuing consequences.

Respect vs. Disrespect

How many times has our young adult said to us that they deserve our respect and because we do not show respect to them, they will not show respect to us?

Because many times and about many things we disagree with the poor choices our problematic young adults make, it would be easy not to respect them as a person in their own right. It is one thing to not respect their actions, it is quite another thing not to respect their right to choose those actions. Of course, their rights end where ours begin when they are not respectful of who we are.

It is important to our self-care, to our relationship with our young adult, and to our attempt to care for and help them, that we find a way of thinking and feeling that allows us to agree with the value of each person while also disagreeing with the way they are living.

You might be thinking that this is simply the old adage of 'hate the sin, love the sinner!' But what I am advocating is not so much a feeling as it is a respect at such a level that we allow our love to give them the right to fail. Even as I write these words, it is hard for me to have such a respect but I still believe it is needed if we can manage to do it!

Acceptance vs. Approval

Many of us are concerned that this level of respect could be viewed by our young adults, as well as others, as approving of their poor choices and irresponsible actions. This concern may cause us to hesitate to show mutual respect. However, there is a big difference between accepting our young adults versus approving of their beliefs or actions.

Not only is the concept of acceptance facilitative in our relationship with our young adults, it is absolutely necessary for coming to grips with how to live our lives as best we can, with them making a mess of theirs. Until we come to accept the truth of the situation, we will continue to deny to ourselves and others our young adult's problems and the cycle will continue. However, as Alcoholics Anonymous and Narcotics Anonymous, etc., say, our healing begins when we accept the truth, with the hope that the truth will lead us to more personal freedom, and to be as happy as we can, despite our young adult's "choice" not to do the same. I use quotation marks around the word "choice" here because sometimes it is no longer a choice, but an illness that is affecting them at such a level that without outside help, they have little choice but to hopefully ask for help.

Hope vs. Hopelessness

Indeed, many times it is very difficult to see any hope, and feelings of hopelessness take over. When this happens, we end up being as or more miserable than our problematic young adult. Day after day, night after night, week after week, month after month, even year after year, go by with sometimes little or no relief in sight. We lose hope or we hope against hope for the pain to let up for our young adults and for us.

No, absolutely not! That's my answer to someone who would say I am being a little melodramatic at this point. Folks, it gets bad, real bad.

So what are we to do to survive? Recognize there is hope! Hopefully, for our young adults but definitely for us as parents. That's part of what I am trying to underscore in the treatment of this whole subject. If we believe in and apply these and other healthy concepts in parenting young adults and in caring for ourselves, then there is hope. If we are not willing to recognize and implement healthy coping concepts, that is our decision much like it is for our young adult and, as

81

is true for them, we must live with our decisions. My hope for all of us is that we will consider doing what we need to do to have hope in our lives even if our young adults are not yet at that place.

Self-Sacrifice vs. Self-care

The title of this book is *Co-deparent No More,* and is primarily focused on self-care while trying to parent problematic young adults. Too often it turns out that parents feel like they are not experiencing self-care at all, but self-sacrifice. There is a tendency for us to blame our young adults for our unhappiness. Many of us feel like the victim.

Learning to take care of ourselves and not expecting our young adults to take care of us equals self-care. Once again I emphasize the need to stop being the victim and to begin taking care of our own lives by being more autonomous (self-governing) and less codependent (unhealthy dependence) on our young adults. Sounds good, doesn't it? Too good to be true, you ask? It is possible to take care of ourselves in such a way that our "misery factor" goes down, enabling us to enjoy life better than we have been.

When talking about self-care, we are not talking about being selfish. At a minimum, we use the formula of "taking as much care of ourselves as we try to take care of our young adults." If we do not take care of ourselves, who will? It is evident that our young adults can't take care of themselves let alone us, so we need to rethink the expectation that they can. When our young adults take responsibility for themselves and make better decisions, that is an extra blessing/perk we can experience, but the foundation of our happiness must rest with our own self-care, not with our young adults.

Empowerment of Self vs. Overpowering Our Young Adults

One way we try to have empowerment in our lives, is to overpower our young adults, or attempt to do so. We do this by trying to force our young adults to be responsible and make better decisions for their life. However, as we pointed out earlier, the authoritarian approach will no longer work. Authority, you say? What authority? Yes, you are correct. The authority we have is the authority in our own lives and if we give it away, there goes any sense of empowerment for ourselves.

When we feel like a victim, are afraid to be even mildly confrontational and either follow the path of least resistance or (and I know it seems contradictory) try to make them act responsibly, the power in our lives belongs to someone else, probably our young adult.

When we decide to reclaim our lives, not let others have the primary say-so, accept responsibility for who we are, how we feel, what decisions we make, and take responsibility for our own happiness, then and only then do we begin to feel a sense of growing empowerment.

If You Will, I Will vs. If You Won't, I Won't

One of the most important 'Ah-Ha' moments is when we become aware that since we go to work every day and our problematic young adults do not, but could, then we are not required to feel bad when our lives have more advantages than theirs do. And in addition to this, we are not required to be responsible for seeing to it that our young adults have the same advantages that we do by footing the bill, especially since they are not doing this for themselves. Why should we go to work every day, month after month and year after year, and give money to our young adults who choose not to work at all? Can we answer the 'Why' to this question? Sure we can- because we feel guilty for our advantages. But wait! Answer me why we feel guilty for working hard every day and earning our advantages and our young adult chooses not to work but could and thus of course, does not have these advantages?

Okay, I'm being a little too hard on us. Because we love our young adults even if they are unmotivated or make poor choices, we naturally have feelings about their plight. So, what's a parent to do?

As the title of this coping concept suggests, we can communicate to our young adults that when they refuse to help themselves, in whatever ways they could, we are not going to help them. But when they are willing to do so, or even try to do their part, we will help them out. Thus, the concept, "If you won't, I won't, but if you will, I will." Again, the decision is up to the young adult! So try not to feel guilty or bad if they decide not to do their part. That decision dictates that we cannot do what we otherwise would without enabling them in their irresponsible behavior.

Healthy Love vs. Unconditional Love

I have heard and read many times that we are to have "unconditional love" for our children. Haven't you? Besides not knowing exactly what this means, I'm also not sure that it is that helpful of a concept (whatever it is). It sounds awfully good, that we have no conditions on our love for our children. And, I would certainly agree that if we can do this (and evidently many can) we would want to.

However, I feel this concept could set up parents and young adults to have an unhealthy relationship, especially if we have problematic or irresponsible young adults. For, in the name of unconditional love, our relationship with our young adults could, and sometimes does, become so confused that we feel no matter how our young adult treats us or others, we have to, in the name of unconditional love, support or back them in their actions. And, if we do not, we do not really love them. "If you really love me, you will do this unconditionally, no matter what!" It is at this very point that I feel we begin to confuse unconditional love with unconditional actions and/or unconditional enabling.

The possibility of making this confusing mistake is why I prefer the concept of healthy love vs. unconditional love. Healthy love involves love of self as well as love of our young adults. Deciding to take care of ourselves by refusing to support or enable our irresponsible young adult is a part of healthy love. The other part of healthy love for our young adults is to explain to them, and hopefully they will hear, that our love for them may be strained by their poor choices and that we may not back their actions, but we do love them deeply even if they don't think we do. This is simply another logical consequence to their actions and the choices they make.

Positive vs. Negative Reinforcement

In the section earlier entitled, "Punishment vs. Natural Consequences", the emphasis was particularly on the negative consequences of our young adults' poor choices and irresponsible behavior.

However, this coping concept emphasizes the rewards that both the young adult and the parent can experience if we as parents will express in various and sundry ways, the rewards that can be theirs (ours) when healthy choices are made and responsible actions take place.

When our young adults make good choices and act responsibly, it is as important to reward them as it is to refuse to enable them when they are acting in unhealthy ways. In fact, it may be even more important.

A reward or positive reinforcement can range from a verbal "good job" to committing oneself to helping them financially or in other creative, positive ways. And, believe me when I tell you, it blesses us probably even more than our young adult, as we get the opportunity to celebrate with them in their good choices, responsible actions, or in realizing a goal successfully met.

Parent vs. Friend

This particular coping concept has to do with the most basic aspect of our relationship with our young adults. By definition our relationships with our young adults is that we are their parent before and even after we are their friend. You might be asking, why make this distinction? I feel we need to be aware of the difference between parent and friend, especially when parenting problematic young adults. This distinction might not be as important when relating to responsible young adults.

The main difference between being a parent and a friend is that, "once a parent, always a parent," as opposed to the idea that friendship can exist, but under certain circumstances it can also end. Sometimes when the going gets rough, the friendship gets gone! But no matter what, we continue to be a parent in good or bad times. We might not act or even feel like a parent and child, but biologically and emotionally we are still bound and are still parent and child. This is part of the reason for the deep pain we can experience when our young adult is extremely unhappy. We are always a parent!

When it is possible to develop a friendship with our young adults, it usually is an indication that we are beginning to have more in common with our problematic young adult and he/she is acting in ways that are more conducive to the birth and growth of a friendship and this is a day to celebrate!

Taking these points into consideration, one can understand the necessity of prioritizing self-care (especially parents of problematic young adults), since we are parents forever. By definition there are no "fair weather" parents, as can be true in some friendships.

Reasonable vs. Unreasonable

The admonition of the Good Book to, "Come now, let us reason together," is indeed a healthy coping concept.* The more reasonable we can be, the better we will take care of ourselves and relate in healthy ways to our problematic young adults.

It is very important that we not get caught up in the irrational thinking and behavior of our young adults and their requests for us to do just that. Reason can give way if we are not grounded.

Acting in unreasonable ways can reflect our lack of a healthy philosophy of parenting and can reveal our true nature.

One of Aesop's fables is that of the scorpion and the frog. The fable is that a scorpion asked a frog to give him a ride on his back to get across the pond. The frog said no since he feared the scorpion would sting him. The scorpion insisted he would not do that because it would be unreasonable. For by stinging him, the frog would die and the scorpion would drown. The frog agreed and the scorpion climbed on. Half way across the pond, the scorpion stung the frog. As they were both sinking into the water, the frog said to the scorpion, "That wasn't a reasonable thing to do." The scorpion replied, "I know it wasn't, it's just my nature to sting."*

Of the various underpinnings of a solid parenting philosophy, one is to try to think and act reasonably, avoiding knee-jerk reactions. Or, important as it is to be in touch with our feelings, it is also important to stop, look, listen and think before we speak, commit, and act, in relationship to our young adults and to our plan of self-care.

Start With Us vs. Start With Young Adults

Speaking of self-care, it is my opinion, unless we take care of ourselves we will not do an adequate job of caring for our needy young adults. As a general rule of thumb we need to start with us and work our way to our young adults. Of course, there are exceptions to this as we well know, but for the most part we need to meet our needs first. You say, "Is this being selfish?" I do not see it as being selfish but as the necessity of self-care and self-nurture. Let's don't kid ourselves, we have needs too. And, if we do not meet our needs, we might require others, including our needy young adults, to take care of us to everyone's detriment. Remember the concept of parentification, addressed earlier, where we require our children to take care of or parent us? Since they can barely care for themselves... well, you get the picture.

No, it is not being selfish to care for ourselves! It is absolutely necessary if we are trying to parent an irresponsible young adult. Instead of wasting our time being hurt, angry and frustrated that our young adults are not meeting our needs by both demonstrating love to us in word or deed and by staying out of serious trouble, we simply need to do those things that demonstrate care for ourselves. Once this basic requirement is met we have a firm foundation for trying to provide much needed care for them.

At the very heart of parenting problematic young adults is the basic requirement of self-care. I again am not saying be selfish, but again, and again, I am stressing the importance of taking care of ourselves so we can be equipped to care for our children, or anyone else for that matter. Thus, the title of this book reflects parental self-care.

One might be wondering if there is a place for sacrifice in parenting problematic young adults since I am advocating care for self first. All I can say is if you are asking this question, you have either never parented an irresponsible young adult, or if you have/are, then you are in very deep trouble.

One additional word on this topic of self-care is that I feel one of the best (if not the best) ways to help our young adult is to model for him/her how to take care of one's self in a healthy way with the hope that they will inquire as to how to do this and a dialogue will open up between us which might lead to their own self-care.

Prioritize vs. Nit-Pick

I'm sure we have all heard the phrase, "Pick your battles." Well my phrase is, "Prioritize your needs, don't nit-pick." We need to spend more serious time assessing the needs we and our young adults have and prioritize what is the very most important, to the least important, to the it doesn't matter anyway. We want to major on the majors, not on the minors. Let the minors go! There is not enough of time, money, or us to cover every base.

Most likely, each one of us will have a different set of priorities. Some, of course, will be very similar. The main thing is that we not go off half-cocked but seriously decide what three or four things are the most important. If we can concentrate on these, we are off to a good start.

In serious situations, the needs boil down to food, shelter and clothing. For others, it might be health issues or legal concerns that are at the top of this list; for others, financial problems and the need for a job—any job. One major problem we might encounter is that what we see as the most important might be different from what our young adult sees as important. It will likely be necessary to work on restating these differences and in most cases, compromising.

Let me remind you that as responsible parents of an irresponsible young adult, we have to be prepared to state what we will or will not do, and not try to tell or make our young adults see it or do it our way. They have a choice to make so try to let them make it and try to let them live with the consequences no matter how serious the implications of their choices are.

If we major on the minors, nit-pick, (for example: the length of their hair, tattoos, the clothes they wear, the music they listen to, etc.) we are not likely to be successful in our parenting endeavor. By the way, what I might see as a minor, you might see as a major. So do your own thing at this point, okay?

Recovering vs. Recovered

Anyone familiar with Alcoholics Anonymous (AA), Narcotics Anonymous (NA), Over-Eaters Anonymous (OA), etc., is familiar with the concept of being in recovery as opposed to being recovered. We might ask though, what's the difference? I answer, all the difference in the world!

To say one is recovered is to say one is fixed or cured. But to say one is in recovery is to say one is making progress in treatment and living successfully with the condition. What condition, you ask? Well, the condition of trying to have a hopeful life as a parent of an irresponsible, problematic young adult.

At this point, one might be getting worried that I'm saying our situation is not fixable. Well, in some ways, this is correct. For, I might ask us the question, is life fixable? My answer is that one does not try to fix life but instead tries to live life as hopefully and successfully as one can. If we were to judge the worth of life by the ultimate outcome, we would lose heart, for as they say, 'none of us get out of here alive.' However, if we judge life, including our efforts in living in recovery with our problematic young adults by the experiences we have, there can be many hopeful minutes, hours, days, and sometimes even weeks, months, and years.

As I write these words, it again reminds me that I am trying to take an honest, realistic look at our condition, and neither a rose-colored glasses nor a pessimistic approach. In fact, it is possible (and has and does happen), that we can go on to be in recovery to live hopeful lives, both us and our young adults. When and if this happens, celebrate, give thanks, and keep it up. However, for others of us who are experiencing recovery day by day, life can still be worth living and for that we too can celebrate, give thanks, and keep it up day by day. As one of the founding fathers of the psychological movement was quoted as saying... "If there is a flower that blooms for only one single night, its bloom does not appear to us on that account any less splendid." *

Different vs. Right or Wrong

Several years ago Joseph Fletcher came up with the concept of "situational ethics." In essence, he said that there was not a set right or wrong in the universe, but it varied as to any given situation. He went on to say that the right thing to do was whatever was the "loving thing to do."**

Well, I'm not an ethicists, but it seems that Dr. Fletcher went out a little too far for me on the ethical limb. Even though I cannot agree on all of his thesis, I do like what he says about doing the loving thing or loving act toward any situation (as far as is humanly possible).

Along a similar line, I feel it is important not to get caught up with our young adults in a debate about who is right and who is wrong. Instead, recognize we both have a different way of looking at responsibilities in life and try in a loving way to state our differences. Just because we have differences, does not have to mean that someone has to be wrong. Also, it does not mean that we have to do it our young adult's way either, especially when we feel it is not the responsible thing to do. In love we can differ even if a compromise cannot be found, without distancing ourselves even more by insisting we are right.

The idea of us and our young adults seeing situations in different vs. right or wrong ways is another type of paradigm that could keep our lines of communication open and our relationships on healthier grounds.

Motivation vs. Manipulation

Speaking of ethics and the loving thing to do, I think we can safely say that trying to manipulate our young adults is not the loving thing to do nor is it the right thing to do. Making efforts to motivate our young adults to be more responsible and make better choices is a loving act.

Using some of the healthy coping concepts we are looking at would be a possible way to motivate our problematic young adults where using unhealthy concepts might fall into the category of manipulation.

The Golden Rule seems applicable at this point. We relate to our young adults like we would want them to relate to us. All of us know how it feels when our young adult tries to manipulate us with guilt, threats, etc., so it stands to reason that our young adults feel similarly when we try to manipulate them. Some of the problems we have in relating is due to their intense resistance to our trying to manipulate them with guilt or threats.

The story is told of the wind and the sun discussing which of them could get a man to take off his coat the quickest. The wind blew and blew, but the more it blew, the tighter the man kept his coat around him. Then the sun came out and slowly warmed up the day. Gradually, the man unbuttoned his coat and took it off.* Let us try to be more like the warm sun than the cold wind.

Compliance vs. Conformity

For many people, and especially for problematic young adults, there seems to be a strong need not to conform but to do it "their way", even if their way is not working for them (or for us). The more they insist on it being their way, the more we are frustrated when their way is causing problems and headaches for all of us. If we are not careful, we will get into a power struggle with them insisting that they conform to our way or else. When this happens, usually more problems develop in our relationship instead of our hope for a positive result coming to fruition.

Instead of insisting on conformity to our way, we work toward the goal of compliance to a workable solution no matter whose way it is, ours, theirs, or some other healthy choice. We are less likely to meet serious resistance and possibly avoid the power struggle if we work toward compliance vs. insisting on conformity. After all, if we do not care who gets the credit as long as the goal is reached, a lot more can be accomplished and we can care for ourselves as well as our young adults in a more successful way.

Trust vs. Mistrust

Erick Erickson said one of the earliest developmental tasks we as humans attempt to accomplish is that of trust. He went on to say that if we are not successful, we experience mistrust. He felt that children as young as one year old begin to experience either a feeling and ability to trust oneself and others or they begin to mistrust life with all its negative implications.*

Of course if we are trying to parent an irresponsible young adult, there usually is very little trust in both directions. We find it difficult to trust our young adult and our young adult finds it difficult to trust us. If we are honest, sometimes we don't even trust ourselves and our own judgment in chronic, painful situations.

As much as we want our young adult to be responsible so we can trust him/her, I feel we need to first start with trying to trust ourselves, our judgment, and the decisions we make in relationship to them. One of the best ways to gain trust in our parenting abilities is to seek the opinion of others about the direction we are taking in trying to deal with a problematic young adult. If we have serious doubts about our trustworthiness and in our decisions, it will be more difficult to trust others, especially our young adults with their serious problems in the areas of being dependable and trustworthy. Seeking the opinions of others who have experience in this field or who at least are mature and dependable can help in many ways. We will feel less pressure and stress; they frequently will "hear" and "heed" unbiased counsel more readily.

Ideal vs. Reality

Most all of us have heard the analogy of the half glass of water. The question is whether it is half full or half empty? In reality it is simply a half glass of water. Whether it is half full or half empty depends on each person's interpretation of their own reality. While one person might see it as half full, another person might see it as half empty. We must come to grips with what we feel is the reality of the issues we and our young adults are dealing with. I am fond of saying the only advantage one has of sticking their head in the sand if a Mack truck is bearing down on them is that they don't see the truck that hits them!

To live our lives as if things are okay when they are not is simply calling a half glass of water half full or burying our head in the sand. On the other hand, to make a mountain out of a mole hill is to "catasrophasize" a situation out of proportion.

Here again, seeking the opinion of a trusted confidant or a good friend whom we feel is level-headed and who preferably has had some experience with parenting young adults, will help in determining the reality of our situation. For, many times we are so close to the situation that we lose objectivity and either under react or over react to everyone's demise.

If we don't have a firm footing in these situations, we will form a misalliance with our irresponsible young adult and unwittingly let them determine the reality of the situation. Most of the time the young adult is the last person we need to be allowing to determine our reality!

Many of us have had the experience of not knowing if we are being too easy or too hard on our young adults. As someone has said, children do not come with a manual ('til now)! Finding ways to determine or measure what is a healthy response to the issues we encounter in trying to take care of ourselves and care for our problematic young adults is extremely important. This is the heart of what I am attempting to do for myself and for other parents who are in similar situations.

Lastly, as a friend of mine said, "We cannot keep our young adults from experiencing the realities all other persons have to experience, including ourselves as parents."

Forgetting vs. Forgiveness

The only thing wrong with the principle 'forgive and forget' is that it is not always possible to forget. It is possible to forgive. I say it is possible to forgive, I did not say it was an easy task nor a certainty by any means.

On some occasions (more than we like to admit), so much hurt and pain has been experienced by all parties that all we seem to have left are attempts at forgiveness—both our need to forgive as well as our need to be forgiven. And, the need for forgiveness is important whether we are able to mend our broken relationship or not. Hopefully, we can salvage our relationships, but if we cannot, we really need to be able to discover forgiveness for our own happiness and peace of mind.

The concept of 'discovering forgiveness' as opposed to the traditional idea of doing forgiveness is an idea I am learning (remember, recovering not recovered) from John Patton's book, *Is Human Forgiveness Possible?** He suggests that as we discover we have more in common with our problematic young adults than we think, especially our imperfections, we come to discover our need to be forgiven too.

In addition to this, I really like what John Claypool says about forgiveness in his book, *Mending the Heart.* To paraphrase Claypool, he says... "Forgiveness is more like the event of birth than anything else. We did nothing whatsoever to be born into this world, for birth is a windfall, and so is forgiveness. Forgiveness is sheer grace and patience and hopefulness which allows us to try again at life even when we have failed...it is that we are more interested in our future than our past, more interested in what kind of person one can yet become than the kind of person we used to be."*

There is another popular saying that 'time heals all things'. Although I don't believe that time can heal all things, I do believe that with the passing of time and with forgiveness, many of our hurts can heal and our broken relationships with our problematic young adults can start and continue the process of recovery. For, life is too short not to try to discover forgiveness if at all possible.

Pain vs. Pleasure

Pain vs. Pleasure, otherwise known as the Reality vs. the Pleasure Principle, is an important concept in understanding some major differences between us and our irresponsible young adults. The Pleasure Principle is where one does what they want to and does not do what they do not want to, with little regard for the consequences. The Reality Principle is where one sometimes (many times in fact) has to delay gratification in order to do what is needed and is mindful of the consequences of their actions.** It is obvious which principle most responsible parents adhere to and which principle most problematic young adults adhere to.

This major difference can explain a lot about why we stay frustrated with our young adults and why it is so difficult to encourage them to do what is needed, not just what is most expedient. This difference can be a partial explanation of why our young adults do what they do in their relationships, their irresponsible spending habits, and many other unhealthy choices they make.

In order to take care of ourselves and try to care for our young adults, we must be aware of these differences and take them into account or we will continue to be unhappy, worried, and frustrated. Recognizing and respecting the fact that if our young adults continue to avoid responsibility and seek immediate gratification, they are choosing this for themselves and we are to be careful not to let them make this same choice for us.

Accountable vs. Not Accountable

The difference between being accountable and not being accountable is the difference between day and night. If we are not willing to ask our young adults to be accountable, for all intents and purposes, we are going to be frustrated and angry with them. Being upset with them is not conducive to our own well-being nor is it conducive to our desired relationship with them.

If our young adults choose not to or cannot be accountable for their actions and choices, we need to come to recognize this and the sooner we do, the less frustrated we can be. To be aware that our young adults are having a big problem in this area can cause us to rethink what we are doing or not doing in relation to them. We can only be accountable to modify our efforts in such a way that we are not as upset, frustrated, and angry with them because there is less we are asking of them and also less we are doing for them. We can be accountable to ourselves to live up to our commitment that when and if they will, we will, and if they choose not to, we will not either. In other words, we get the monkey off of our back or the ball out of our court. After that, what that monkey does with that ball is no longer up to us!

Helping vs. Hurting

At the very heart of the treatment of this whole subject is the profound desire we have to help, not hurt, our irresponsible young adults. If we use this principle alone to inform our decisions, words, and actions (or lack thereof), I believe the intent of this book would, more times than not, be fulfilled. That is, we could avoid being as unhappy as our unhappiest child and just might avoid enabling them in ways that hurt instead of help. And, as stated earlier, if we are not clear about this, seek informed words from a trusted source as to the possible consequences of our efforts to help. Remember, most of the time we cannot depend on our problematic young adults to counsel us about this. Also remember we have to be prepared not to let their response to our intended helpful decisions influence us in such a way that we collude with them in helping them down a hurtful path of more problems. To give in to our fears of what our young adults are going to think of us for not "helping" them might very well end up hurting them. Again, this points to the fact that we need to have our act together or we both will be hurt in the long run. Let us take courage and again go back to the basic principle of our commitment to help our young adults even if, at the time, it makes us uncomfortable and can be just plain hard to do.

Single Message vs. Double Message

Years ago when Johnny Carson hosted The Tonight Show, frequently as he came out on stage to begin his monologue, while the audience was wildly applauding, with his right hand raised, he would motion for them to stop applauding and at the same time, with his left hand lowered by his side, he would be motioning for them to keep it up! Remember that? Well, when Johnny did this, it was all in fun, but when we as parents do a similar thing with our irresponsible young adults, it is not at all funny. If we send mixed signals to them, we become partly responsible for the confusion that follows. When we are able to send a clear message in an assertive way, we have lived up to our responsibility for ourselves and our responsibility to our young adults.

Another way to say this is to let our yeas be yea and our nays be nay and to clearly signal only one at a time.

What We Can Do vs. What We Cannot Do

It is important that we don't let what we cannot do keep us from what we can do. Many times we expend lots of energy, money and time trying to do what we cannot do. It is very important to save our efforts to apply to the things we can do.

Taking a second look at the healthy coping concepts previously addressed could help determine the best areas to invest our efforts. Each one of these concepts has a side that one would find is like the "black hole." There seems to be no light at the end of that endless tunnel. To spend our efforts with these would be like spinning our wheels. (All we get in return for all our efforts is to go round and round only to find ourselves deeper stuck in the quagmire of trying to help our irresponsible young adults!) This leaves us even more disheartened, discouraged, angry and sometimes even broke, and our young adult is in no better place than when we started.

To use our efforts in doing what we can, might be to choose the other side of these healthy coping concepts. Even though there are no guarantees, one is much more likely to see positive results of our investments. And even though the result might be less than we'd hoped for, remember, something is better than nothing. This is particularly true when we have tried to do what we cannot do. Plus, this side of the positive vs. negative choice can sometimes at least help us take care of ourselves while hoping to see some progress for our young adults.

It is not so much a matter of success or failure but the fact that our good intentions do count when they are based on healthy decisions. We also need to realize that we cannot judge our success by what our young adults do with their choices in life. We are accountable for only what we do with our choices and for recognizing what we can and cannot do to help our young adults.

Our Life vs. Their Life

Let me ask you a question. As a parent of an irresponsible young adult do you sometimes feel that you have no life of your own? I'm going to bet the farm that I know the answer to that question. I am about to show you just how good I am and say what you are thinking right now..."What life?"

It is easy to lose ourselves in all the troubles of our young adults. Remember we discussed earlier that if we do not have a solid sense of self, of our own individuality and ability to separate self from young adults, we will probably become codependent on them? When we become codependent, we lose our own life in direct proportion to that dependency. Because we love them so much and are worried to death about them, it is natural that we forget what our needs are and concentrate first and foremost on their needs and their life.

It is primary to remember who we are and who they are. Since it is a full-time job just trying to live our own lives, it is a little presumptuous to try to live theirs, too. Because we forget that we cannot fix life, only live it, we slip into not recognizing the boundary that defines who each individual person is.

The title of the T.V. show, "One Life to Live," is a very poignant phrase. We each only have the ability and power to live one life in a lifetime—our own. We hope that the example we set, the choices we make, and the influence we have on others will be positive and rewarding. And, I might add, living one life in a lifetime is plenty for me!

Letting Go vs. Not Letting Go

There seems to be two aspects to this concept. One is that we have trouble letting go of our young adults so they can go on to live their own lives; the concept called "the empty nest syndrome" reflects this particular dynamic. When our young adults leave home, they sometimes take with them too much of us. We have been so involved with them that we have neglected to develop other interests and our lives feel empty without them. This possibly can be a reflection of the lack of investment we have in our spouse or significant others in our lives. When our young adults are irresponsible, due to their troubled teenage years, we feel they are unprepared to start out on their own and naturally worry about them to the point that we cannot let go.

The other side of this concept is reflected in the title of the movie, "Failure to Launch." The theme of this movie reflects that we want to let go so our young adults can start out on their own life, separate from us, but the young adults are not prepared to, or choose not to leave the nest. Thus, we have a failure to launch. Also, there is another aspect to reckon with as baby boomer parents, the "boomerang" effect. That is when the young adult launches, but returns to the roost by nightfall! He/she underestimates what it takes to live out in the old, cold world and cannot make it on their own, so they return to the warmth of the nest, unless they convince us to bankroll their "independence." If we do this over a consistent period of time, I feel it is not help to our young adults in the long run and painfully drains us in every way.

Here again, it is up to us to be prepared. If we are not prepared, it is up to us to get prepared, or at least try to. The preparation started all the way back to the time our little girl or boy began school. It is that very moment that we experienced the separation anxiety that comes with our little ones being on their own, even for a few hours a day. The more successful we were back then, the more we and our young adults will be ready, prepared and equipped to launch and not return to the nest except for family and fun visits.

Black Sheep vs. Family Problem

In Family Systems theory, we talk about the 'identified patient' better known as the 'black sheep' of the family.* The temptation is/can be for a family to compare themselves to the black sheep and perceive themselves snow white, when in reality there is no black sheep or white sheep, only gray. The identified patient is a reflection of the dysfunction that many times we see in the family as a whole unit. Some professionals in this field even go as far as to say the identified patient in some ways is trying to get help for all of us.

You know where I stand on this point. Right? I feel we all need help. That is why I say we need self-care and attention as well as do our troubled young adults, and that the starting and finishing point is with us. This will assure that we are more prepared to try to help them in healthy ways, not in co-dependent ways, not enabling their poor choices, but by being assertive in letting them know where we stand.

Front End vs. The End

By now, you are probably way past ready for these Healthy Coping Concepts to come to an end. Well, actually we have come to an end, the "front end" of a process that has no end! Say what? As Kathy Peel says in her book, *Family for Life*, " we are forever the parents of our children"*...irresponsible or not.

For this reason, it is wise for us to pace ourselves. Our self-care is even more consequential in that it is a life-long process. A commitment to use healthy coping skills to relate to our young adults is essential.

Even though there are always exceptions as to where one must concentrate in the moment to help in a crisis, most of our efforts must be balanced between the here and now and the then and there. If we are not careful, we will get caught up in the here and now in which our problematic young adults live, compounding the pain. One of the jobs as parents is to be able to see past the gratification and even the necessity (according to our young adults) and delay the gratification or quick fix for the more solid long term response. This long term response is in reality a necessity for us even if our young adults do not view it the same way we do.

In concluding this chapter, it is worthwhile to realize that one does not come to implement these Healthy Coping Concepts overnight. It is a commitment to start and continue to develop and grow toward what we feel in our heart and head is the best approach to a very complicated set of pivotal concepts and coping skills. Hopefully, as we implement some of these concepts in our particular situations and circumstances, life can be better for us and our relationships with our young adults can be healthy too.

<u>The Reader's Page</u>

The Reader's Page

The Reader's Page

Chapter 5

Effects on Our Marital Relationship

In some ways, this chapter needed to be at the first of this book. Before any children are present to bless us and worry us to death, we as a couple exist. Before we are mother and father, we are husband and wife. And, when our children, as young adults, set out on their own, leave our home for their own home (hopefully), we as a couple still exist (hopefully)! The whole process begins and ends with the two of us. Therefore, the effects this has on us as individuals and as a couple are very important.

There are a number of issues that can be either problematic or facilitative in their effects on our marriage. One such is that even though we are married, we still are individuals first and foremost.

When we both are in agreement as to how to relate to our problematic young adults and we present a solid front, then two positive things can occur. First, we as an individual, personally feel okay about the healthy way we are relating to our young adults. As the old saying goes, the one whose opinion counts the most is the one looking back at us in the mirror. As difficult and sometimes heart-wrenching as it is to make healthy choices when dealing with the problems our irresponsible young adults have, to be able to feel personally, in our heart of hearts, that we are doing what we feel to be the best of all the options in front of us, will allow us to sleep, at least a little better, than we otherwise would.

Secondly, when each of us as individuals, both wife and husband, are on the same page, it can strengthen our relationship as a couple and therefore our marriage. Even if we are not on the same paragraph (which seldom we are) if we are on the same page, we as a couple can remain healthy, even though, sometimes our efforts don't produce the same positive results for our hurting young adults.

Another issue is a negative result(s) that will possibly develop when we do not agree on the approach to take with our troubled young adults. This can lead to unhappiness on the part of us as an individual and as a couple. In extreme situations we can experience serious anxiety and depression as individuals and marriage threatening problems as a couple. Thus, when a couple cannot agree as to what ways to relate to their young adults, not only are the young adults not benefited, the couple is sometimes even more unhappy than their young adults. (Which you know by now is a major premise of this book.)

Once again, it is not being selfish for parents of troubled young adults to begin with themselves; this is self care. Each parent as an individual, must work toward self-care, as well as together as a couple. This is a necessity in order to keep our marital relationship on solid footing. In discussing this with someone, he pointed out to me that this is certainly an appropriate and healthy place for a couple to "put their oxygen mask on first and then attempt to help their trouble young adult put his/her oxygen mask on."

Volumes have been written as to the effects on our marriage when we seriously disagree as to the parenting of our children, young and old, responsible or not. However, there are unique stresses particular to a marriage relationship when we are discussing parenting problematic young adults. To underestimate these unique concerns can put the very foundation of our family in jeopardy. Thus, I feel it is essential that every effort be made to be sensitive to what makes marital self-care effective and what simultaneously makes parenting of our troubles young adults more effective.

The Reader's Page

The Reader's Page

Chapter 6

Effects on Other Members of the Family

On the Larry King Live television show, Mr. King had as his special guest, Mr. Art Linkletter. In his interview with Mr. Linkletter, they discussed the topic of the tragic death of Mr. Linkletter's grown daughter after years of a troubled life. Mr. King asked Mr. Linkletter how he, "...kept from going crazy after his daughter's death?" Mr. Linkletter replied, "It would have been easy to go crazy, but my other children did not deserve a crazy father."*

The above scenario, in a very poignant way, points to the effects that a troubled life of a young adult can have on other members of the family, including the siblings of problematic young adults. This is piercingly true if the other siblings have led or are leading a responsible life. The energies we invest in the troubled young adult can have a negative effect on these well adjusted siblings and their efforts. Mr. Linkletter in essence said that it would have been easy to invest himself in his daughter and her problems so intensely that there would have been none of him left for his other children.

If we don't stop and think, not just feel and act, we can deplete our resources on the troubled young adult and have little, if anything, left to share with other children. These depleted resources can include, but are not limited to, emotional energy, financial resources, hours, days, weeks, and years of invested time, the physical and mental health of parents, a troubled and/or loss of a marriage and home, legal involvements, and other lost resources that the members of the family need for their livelihood.

There is a saying that the squeaky wheel gets the grease. In this particular setting, there is usually a lot of squeaking going on from the problematic young adult. It seems quite natural as a parent, without stopping and thinking, to respond to the needs of our children. Isn't that what a good parent does? My answer is that in some situations we do need to move quickly to help out in a crisis. However, in the case of one crisis after another over an extended period my answer is that there needs to be a balance between thinking and feeling before we act to use or use up our resources with our troubled young adult. In this case, a healthy parent might need to say NO. This is critical when we have other children who use, not misuse the resources we invest in their lives in a constructive not destructive way. Remember, "No" does not mean that we do not love our irresponsible young adult or that we love our responsible young adult more. Sometimes the most loving thing we can do is say "No" and stick to it with all its positive and painful ramifications.

A classic example of this is found in the Judeo/Christian story of the wayward son. This particular parent was a farmer who had two sons. The younger son asked for his inheritance while the father was still living because he was tired of being responsible and working on the farm. The wise father complied and the son took the money given him and launched out on his own. After some time of acting irresponsibly, the son spent all his resources, the "boomerang" effect kicked in, and he returned home asking for forgiveness. The story goes on to say the father was glad to see him and threw a big party for his return. At this point, the older more responsible son was upset by the reception and celebration. After all, he had stayed home and worked on the farm and now all this partying was going on for the return of his wayward brother. Sharing his feelings with his father (which seemed appropriate feelings to me) his father responded in his wise and loving way. He told his son that he loved him as well as his younger brother. He said his love for them was not dependent on their actions, but on their value as his two precious sons. He assured his responsible son that the farm belonged to him and that if his brother wanted to stay home he would stay as an employee, but as a loved, forgiven member of the family. The father had not overlooked the dedication of his older son.*

The implication here was that the younger brother would be left to experience the natural or logical consequences of his previous actions. And, no, he would not again receive what he had once asked for and squandered due to his poor choices and irresponsibility. As I understand the moral of this story, the father chose to recognize his commitment to the older son and he also would experience the natural, positive consequences of his responsible decisions.

The Reader's Page

<u>The Reader's Page</u>

Chapter 7

Single Parent Family Issues

As difficult as it is dealing with problematic young adults when we have a partner to help us out, all the more so are the difficulties when we are a single parent. Even if we have an ex spouse or ex significant other to work with us it is still at best extremely stressful. Stressful on our time, our financial resources, our physical and emotional energy, etc.

In many situations one's ex is not that helpful. The problem that led to the relationship ending usually causes a serious breakdown in the communication and cooperation between the two parents. Sometimes one's ex refuses to help the other parent and even makes things worse in trying to parent the troubled young adult because of their strong negative feelings from the divorce or dissolution of the relationship.

There are even times that the disgruntled parent deliberately refuses to help the other parent and seems to take delight in the problems and pain his/her ex is experiencing in relation to trying to help their troubled young adult. (By the way, one can see some of what might be behind the problems of the young adult when one or both parents have these sorts of issues.)

The kind and degree of burdens a single parent experiences when trying to make it on their own along with trying to help their problematic young adult, is a heavy burden indeed. Many of us as single parents have had many a sleepless night worrying ourselves nearly to death over the financial, or legal, or medical, or relational, or ethical, or emotional problems that seem to have no end as it relates to our troubled son or daughter.

I realize what I have been describing is quite a somber and serious situation for a single parent of an irresponsible young adult, but I assure you that if you have ever been in this situation you will agree that all of what I am saying and even more is in fact, fact!

Well then, what are we to do that is in our control as single parents? First, we begin with trying to take better care of ourselves. It is evident that neither our ex or our young adult can or will help us out, so we must try to do what we can that is best for us as a person. In the chapter on "Healthy Coping Concepts" there was an emphasis on self-care. Remember, self-care is not a selfish act; it is a responsible act and even more of a necessity for a single parent since we do not have a partner to help us out.

Secondly, if possible, try to put the differences aside and work with one's ex for the best interest of the troubled young adult. There are some situations where we can appeal to our ex to work together and instead of pulling in separate directions, pull together for the best interest of all concerned.

Thirdly, if our ex will not work with us, we can try to enlist the help and support of other family members or close friends, especially if they have gone through a similar situation. Remember, we do not always have to invent the wheel again if others have had experience in this area.

Fourthly, utilize some of the professionals who are trained in these self-care and parenting situations. By contacting a counselor, a minister, a doctor, etc., one can many times get the much needed support and expertise that will help.

If you or I become aware of a single parent family with a troubled young adult we, too, can possibly be of help. And, one of the best ways to help is by sharing some of the ideas in this book that you found helpful for your situation. As they apply them to their particular circumstances, they also may benefit.

The Reader's Page

The Reader's Page

Chapter 8

Blended Family Concerns

Some while back, when I did my internship and residency at Georgia Baptist Hospital in Atlanta, there existed Fulton County Stadium. In this stadium, two sports teams played their games. One was the Atlanta Falcon football team and the other was the Atlanta Braves baseball team. As I said, both were sports teams, both had many of the same fans attending, they used the same field and the same turf, and the hotdogs and drinks were the same. If one was not careful, one might assume that everything was the same. Not so!

When we take a closer look, we see that the ball they used was different, the number of players was different, the size and shape of the field was different, and most importantly, the rules of the game were different; similar but not the same.

The differences and similarities of a blended family and a non-blended family are analogous to the differences between a football team and a baseball team. In order to be successful as a blended family one must recognize this and relate in ways that reflect such. By the way, I am defining a blended family as one in which at least one of the parents is a step-parent, possible both are step-parents.

Having said this, we as blended family parents of problematic young adults, whether our biological children or our step-children, have a similar but different set of concerns. Just as in football and baseball, the same rules, dynamics and other issues, do not always apply or work. It is therefore necessary to learn some additional parenting and self-care skills peculiar to a blended family. Where some of the dynamics are similar, it is necessary to apply them geared toward the blended family.

There are a number of important dynamics that we need to be sensitive to. As usual, I want to begin with how we as individual parents and as a married couple feel and relate to each other and our problematic young adults. We must recognize that our knowledge of, experience with, and relationship to our biological versus our step-children is different. One is not better or worse, but it is different. This difference is not a good or bad thing but it is a dynamic that exists. If we as a couple are not aware of these dynamics and the implications of them, we can easily accuse our partners of not having the same investment to help with their step-young adults as with their biological young adults. We may incorrectly place value judgments on each other because of these differences as opposed to seeing them simply as differences and working together to help care for our young adults and for our own happiness as a couple.

As in a non-blended family, even more so in a blended family, these problems of our young adults can divide and conquer us. Therefore, our communication with each other is even more important. In fact, all of the "Healthy Coping Concepts" previously addressed, the effects on our marriage, and the effects on step-brothers and sisters in a blended family, present even more of a challenge than to non-blended families.

Since it is not my purpose at this point to be exhaustive as to the peculiar issues facing blended families, I'll limit my discussion to a few important issues. Because of the difference in the knowledge of, experience with, and relationship to step-young adults, versus our biological children, we are many times more defensive about our biological young adults and more critical of our step-children. Our defensiveness is also frequently driven by our guilt over our part in the problems our irresponsible young adults have due to the fact of the "failure" of the family he or she was born into. Remember at this point the two things we said about guilt. One is that many times underneath guilt is grief and sadness and as we work through our grief at a failed marriage and its effects on our problematic young adults we can parent with less guilt and less grief. This will help us see our parenting skills in a healthier way. The second thing is not to participate in toxic guilt. Yes, we are not perfect parents and yes, we have contributed to some of the problems our young adults experience and for that we do accept our part. However, to so over react to our imperfections that we are driven to parent with toxic guilt is not healthy. This leads to over-compensating in parenting our problematic young adults which is not helping them at all. Our spouse also sees what we are doing and sometimes misinterprets this as preferential treatment to our biological child instead of over-compensating for what we interpret as our "failure." To be aware of this can not only improve parenting of our biological young adult and our step-young adult, but can help keep our relationship with our spouse on a more solid footing.

Another extremely important dynamic that we experience in blended families is resentment that one parent feels toward the other parent if they are expected to say or do something to their biological child that their heart is not in, or that they are not yet ready to say or do. Often we seem more prepared to set limits and say no to our step-child than to our problematic biological young adult, again reflecting the difference in the knowledge, experience, and relationship with them.

To expect our spouse to apply one of the "Healthy Coping Concepts" to their biological young adult when they are not prepared to do so can leave them sad and worried as an individual and can injure the marital relationship. If we are aware of this and take time to process our feelings, we stand a better chance of accomplishing our goal with our irresponsible young adult as well as keeping our marriage in healthier shape. In some extreme cases it can even save our marriage.

<u>Footnote:</u> I would like to suggest the following for us to consider and debate. Unless we have something good to say about our step-children, it's best to say nothing at all. And, listening twice as much as we talk concerning our step-children could save a lot of misunderstanding and heartache.

The Reader's Page

The Reader's Page

Chapter 9

Issues Related to Grandchildren

Charlie Shedd, a noted author of children's books, has been quoted as saying "...and God made grandparents and He said that's very good."* Indeed it is very good to be a grandparent and to have the wonderful opportunity to know, love, and enjoy our grandchildren. The flip side of that coin is the extreme worry, heartache and helplessness a grandparent feels when our irresponsible young adult is not taking good care of the grandchildren due to the problems in their lives. What's a grandparent to do? What can a grandparent do? What, if any, recourses and resources are available to us as grandparents? How can we help our hurting grandchild?

As much as we love our children, problems or not, even more does our heart go out to our helpless grandchildren when they become the victims of the poor choices that our problematic young adults make. It is one thing to not be able to help our young adults who could help themselves, but quite another thing to not be able to help our grandchildren who cannot help themselves. The statement that if we are not careful we will not be any happier than our unhappiest child is even more true when referring to our grandchild!

When we are not autonomous enough and are too codependent to apply healthy coping concepts to our problematic young adults, then it is quite possible that our grandchildren will suffer the consequences of their parents' problems and our difficulties in helping the problem. Thus, one of the greatest motivations for us to act in healthy ways toward our young adults is our grandchildren.

There are very few states where grandparents have any legal rights except for those times grandparents take it on themselves to hire an attorney and attempt to get custody, or temporary custody of their grandchildren. This is usually an uphill battle from the beginning 'till the end and is costly in every way but one. The payoff, if this route is necessary and successful, is the well-being of the grandchild. The peace of mind that we as grandparents have can also be quite rewarding. As difficult as it is to take this route, it is sometimes an absolute necessity for the physical and emotional safety of our precious grandchildren.

Hopefully, the above legal solutions to these problems can be avoided if we can relate in healthy ways with them in parenting their children and our grandchildren. As usual, it is important to begin initially with us as individuals, then as a couple, and lastly working with our problematic young adults.

First, begin by being prepared and ready to share with our young adults what we will and will not do in relation to their unhealthy parenting skills. Our objective is to control ourselves not to try to control our young adults. In assertively sharing this with them, it is hoped they will cooperate with us and allow us to help them be better parents and not enable them in their poor choices where their children are involved. We also have to be prepared for them to be upset with us if it comes to taking more assertive measures for the well-being of the grandchildren.

Secondly, we as grandparents must be on the same page in order to be successful in these endeavors. If we are not pulling together concerning these issues they can pull us apart as a couple. Once we are pulled apart as a couple there is not much we can do to help the situation our grandchildren are in. This makes agreeing as best we can on our approach to these problems essential.

Finally, we as individuals and as a couple need to be prepared to apply healthy ways of relating with the goal in mind of salvaging our relationship with our young adults, but not at the expense of the health and welfare of our grandchildren.

When our grandchildren are being exposed to unhealthy and even dangerous conditions due to the irresponsible parenting skills of our young adults, we must do what we can to help the helpless. If there comes a time when we have to let the chips fall where they may, we hope they will fall in ways that are redeemable. If not, we still have to do all we can to see to it our grandchildren have a chance at a safe and healthy life.

Footnote: You might be thinking as a parent of a troubled young adult that either you do not want to raise your grandchildren or you cannot do so for a number of reasons, such as your health concerns, finances and other complications. This is understandable. I'm not suggesting we do so. What I am suggesting is that we do what we can to help all we can these little folks who cannot help themselves.

__The Reader's Page__

_____

_____

_____

_____

_____

_____

_____

_____

_____

_____

_____

_____

_____

_____

_____

_____

_____

_____

_____

_____

Chapter 10

Professional Help

Have you ever been in a situation where in the middle of the intersection your car motor shut off and you couldn't get it started? What a helpless feeling. Right? Then out of the blue some good Samaritan gave you a hand and helped you push your car to the side of the road. What a relief!

Well, we all can use a hand every now and then (I know I can). One of the times most of us can use some assistance and support is in dealing with our problematic young adults. Even though this book is a type of self-help resource, I feel it is important to say that in some cases we need the experience and expertise of a professional resource.

One important source of professional help is Mental Health Counselors. Mental Health Counselors come in all shapes and sizes (in more ways than one). They are available to assist us in taking care of ourselves while trying to care for and help our problematic young adults and their families. The protocol for using the services of a Mental Health Counselor is to first call for an appointment. Explain to him or her the situation and individually or as a couple (which I recommend) go and the three of you decide on a plan of action that might help reach your goal(s). Even though seeing a professional counselor is no guarantee of success, one is more likely to have more success especially if our situation is extremely complicated and serious.

I once heard the story of a farmer who was taking his vegetables to market on a mule-pulled wagon. When he started across a swollen stream, his wagon got stuck in the mud. His mules could not pull him out and his vegetables were in danger of ruining, creating a financial disaster for him. About that time a man came along in a log truck, went across the stream and stopped on the other side. The man asked the farmer if he wanted him to pull his wagon out with his truck. The farmer said yes and the venture was successful. Before the man drove off, the farmer gave him some fresh vegetables for helping and told him if he ever came across him and his truck stuck in the mud he would hitch his mules to the truck and pull him out. And, if he could not pull him out of the mud, he would get in the cab of his truck and sit with him until they could figure out what to do. This scenario exemplifies what a Mental Health Counselor would do. If one cannot immediately help our complicated situation, he or she will sit with us until, together, we can figure out what to do or who to contact for help.

When the young adult is agreeable and willing to go with us to seek the assistance of a professional, we have an even greater chance of helping our situation. There are many reasons for this, not the least of which is that the professional has a chance to make a mental health assessment of our troubled young adult. This is important if our young adult is suffering from a serious emotional condition that could limit his or her abilities to think and act in reasonable ways. If this is the case, our young adult can receive the medical, psychological and/or psychiatric help which will assist them in relating in healthier ways. This is extremely critical if we are worried that our young adult might harm herself/himself. We can use these professional resources to possibly help prevent this, plus, we then can have more assurance that the limits we set will not be too much for him or her to handle. In addition, seeing a professional as a family provides all involved with a safe and supportive environment in which to work on and work out problems together.

Besides Mental Health Counselors, there are other professionals who can help and be a part of the team. Just to mention a few: physicians, psychiatrists, psychologists, social workers, ministers, priests, rabbis, marriage and family counselors, professional counselors, and pastoral counselors, etc.

The Reader's Page

The Reader's Page

Chapter 11

Boomer Co-Deparents' Alanonymous Support Groups

NO! It's not a type-o! I'm suggesting that those of us baby boomers who are trying to take better care of ourselves while trying to parent problematic young adults might consider participating in an Alanonymous Support Group. I know you are saying, "A what kind of group and for whom?"

I will begin by saying that a boomer co-deparent is a baby boomer or any parent who has a codependent relationship with his/her irresponsible young adult 18 years and older. The idea here involves either self-help, leaderless support groups much like AA, NA, OA, etc., or professionally led support groups made up of parents of irresponsible young adults led by a counselor. During some of these meetings, parents work on their own problems and issues that interfere with them relating in healthy ways with their young adults, (like being codependent), thus, the anonymous meeting times. During other meetings, parents work on how to take care of themselves in relation to young adults who have serious problems themselves, (learn to be autonomous), thus the alanon meeting times. The point being that we as parents of problematic young adults need both. We need to work on our own issues sometimes and know how to take care of ourselves in relation to our young adults with problems, as is the case throughout this book. I believe the starting place is with responsible parents working on our issues and taking care of ourselves, then and only then, trying to be of help to our young adults. If we do not begin with getting help for ourselves first instead of trying to help the problematic young adult, we are putting the proverbial cart before the horse.

These groups can vary in their format. They can be on-going groups with parents coming on board as their needs arise or leaving the group as their needs are met. At any given time the participants will be at different places in their circumstance and journey of self-care. Some will have just begun the journey, others will be well on their way, and others will be totally confused and not sure of what to do next.

Another possible format for these groups can be a time limited group with all participants starting and finishing together, and as needed, another group can begin. For example, the group could meet each Tuesday night 7:00-9:00 pm for six weeks.

Whether the groups are leaderless groups or professionally led, or whether they are on-going, time   limited, or some combination of such, one suggestion would be to use the information in this book as a discussion guide for the Alanonymous Meeting Group times. This is one of the reasons I have designed this book to meet our and our problematic young adults' specific needs by leaving some blank pages for you and me as work sheets to personalize our unique situations. And, as we share our particular situation with others in the support group, we will come to see that we can learn from each other.   We can try to do what it seems so hard for our young adults to do--learn from others in similar situations what seems to work or not work for them.

Another format would be to plan a Boomer Co-deparents' Alanonymous Retreat Weekend where a group of concerned parents would spend Friday night through Sunday morning participating in a retreat, working through the ideas and concepts in this book. Organizations such as churches, synagogues, other religious institutions, community based organizations, and corporate sponsorship, etc., can help with organizing, publicizing and expenses of the retreat. For example, an employer could offer this to their employees who need assistance in their lives.

I underscore the fact that there are literally millions and millions of us facing the challenges of trying to help our irresponsible young adults. It is important to share our knowledge with as many others like us as we can, thus, the idea of groups. A key factor is that the support we all need and can benefit from is best done with parents supporting each other in this challenging endeavor.

Incidentally, it does not matter what these groups are called as long as they are effective in helping us and us helping (or trying to help) our young adults. I gave these groups a name. What would you suggest?

<u>Footnote</u>: I begin my Alanonymous Support Groups by saying – "Hi, I'm Murphy. I'm a recovering co-deparent!"

The Reader's Page

Chapter 12

Religion, Self-Care and Parenting

I would not be true to my own religious convictions if I did not say a word or two (or three) about the place one's spiritual beliefs and faith has in this whole process of caring for ourselves while trying to care for our problematic young adults.

I have found that the biggest surprise of my life so far has been my becoming a parent. I did not, nor could not, have imagined in my wildest dreams (and I've had some wild ones) all it means to be a parent. The depth of this role in my life seems deeper than I can express, and that is really deep! If you are a parent (and even more so if you are a grandparent) you know what I mean, right? I have reached the conclusion that being a parent is a spiritual dynamic, not just a biological, relational, and social one.

From my set of beliefs, assumptions, and presuppositions I've also concluded that of all of the disciplines we live with, the deepest are our religious and spiritual beliefs, whatever that might mean to you. And, from my Judeo-Christian perspective, this means a spiritual belief in God. I understand our personal religious faith might be different or one might not be professed at all. This is a position that we all need to respect in others and it is hoped you will give me that respect, too.

Having said this, I go on to say that one of the greatest joys one can experience is the birth of a child or grandchild. As in the words of the hymn, "How sweet to hold a new born baby and feel the pride and joy it gives." *

However, some of the most intense pain and hours of worry can come when that precious child is irresponsible, makes poor decisions and has a pattern of life that is unhealthy and even dangerous.

Since I am not familiar enough with other world religions, I can only speak about the Christian religion with some assurance. What little I do know of other faiths, it is clear to me that there are also similar helps in relationship to our self-care and parenting as we see in the Christian faith.

Because I take a holistic approach to life, that of mind, body and spirit, I and others can receive some guidance from theology as well as psychology, and/or the blending of the two disciplines, in caring for ourselves as parents and in trying to care for and help our troubled young adults.

We might begin with the 'concept of readiness.' Are we (am I) ready to think in ways and make choices about our self-care in relationship to our problematic young adult that we have not done before, realizing that the implications of these decisions might indeed help us achieve the positive goals we have long hoped for?

Robert Havighurst, developmental theorist, spoke of the "right time" or "teachable moment" in this way: "When the body is ripe, and society requires, and the self is ready to achieve a certain task, the teachable moment has come".* However, I believe the concept of readiness is more than this in that it involves a spiritual component also.

An example of what I mean by the concept of readiness that could bring positive results is the biblical story of a man whose legs had been paralyzed for forty years. There was a belief in those days that once a year an angel came and stirred the spring waters at a certain well and whoever dipped in the spring first, would be healed. For forty years the man crawled to the well but was never able to enter the water first. The story goes on to say the man lay despondent after all the crowd had left and he had once again failed to be healed. At this point Jesus and his entourage arrived at the well to have a drink of water. Seeing the man, Jesus asked the people with him what was wrong with the man. They explained his forty year effort to be healed and his inability to reach his goal. At this point, Jesus sat down by the man and asked him the "readiness" question, "Do you want to be healed?" Or, are you ready to be healed, or are you prepared to be healed? **

Being ready to try and think of our relationship with our troubled young adults in ways other than we have before and being ready to relate to them in these new ways can be quite a challenge indeed. It is very important that we be prepared to live with the consequences both positive and negative. We might actually be better prepared to face the negative than the positive results of our different approach to the problems at hand!

You say, what? Was the paralyzed man ready to walk with all that walking entails and are we ready to have a healthier relationship with our young adults with all that entails? Simply put, are we ready for our prayers to be answered? In this man's case he was and he walked away, grateful.

Both psychologically and theologically are we ready to begin to let go of our efforts to try to make our young adults be responsible and have faith/trust in a process that hands over that responsibility to them for their own lives? Are we ready to stop doing some of the things we have done for so long and allow the young adults to start doing these for themselves? And are we ready to begin to apply some healthier ways of relating to our grown children and also begin to apply healthier self-care concepts and actions for ourselves as parents?

Because it is a change from what we have done for so long, it therefore is "risky business" and we are filled with a mixture of doubts, fears, and hopes. That is why faith is needed. Faith, that in time we will begin to see some positive changes take place; faith in our intentions and actions to help in some different ways than before; faith in the personhood of our young adults to begin to respond with better choices and positive results for their lives; and finally, faith that God will participate in this whole process of change and healing in ways only known to Him.

Until one is ready and prepared to go down this road, I've concluded it is best to wait until we can answer the readiness question by saying we indeed want to begin healing personally and have our relationship with our young adult to begin to heal too. We must be ready to begin the process of relating in healthier ways while taking better care of ourselves.

Being realistic however, we need to also face the fact that even though we are ready to begin to make some positive changes in how we relate to our troubled young adults there is no guarantee that they will be prepared or able to do so.

As acknowledged before, some of the most painful situations we can encounter happen when our young adults are making decisions that are bringing serious negative consequences to their lives and leaving us feeling helpless and alone.

In such discouraging times, I've found my faith in God to be helpful. Not necessarily helpful in that the situation is "fixed" but helpful in that I can find comfort and courage to continue to do the best I can in spite of the circumstances.

One way of explaining what I mean can be seen in a statement that Joseph Campbell made to Bill Moyers in the book, *The Power of Myth.* Moyers writes, "Once, as we were discussing the subject of suffering, he (Campbell) mentioned in tandem James Joyce and Igjugarjuk. Who is Igjugarjuk I said, barely able to imitate the

173

pronunciation? Oh, replied Campbell, he was the Shaman of a Caribou Eskimo tribe in northern Canada, the one who told the European visitors that the only true wisdom lives far from mankind, out in the great loneliness and can be reached only through suffering. Privation and suffering alone open the mind to all that is hidden to others." * In essence, all is not lost when our efforts to help are not received in a way that we see positive changes, but instead things continue in a destructive way or even get worse. At these times what we go through, "privation and suffering," can inform us in such a way that we come to realize we can only do so much and that can leave us with a sense of peace about our limitations.

Again, a lesson drawn from the *Bible* illustrates this point quite well. The story goes that nearing the end of Jesus' life while visiting with friends a woman interrupted their meal and poured an expensive bottle of perfume on Jesus' feet. Those closest to Jesus were upset not only at what the woman had done but also that Jesus had allowed her to do so. At this point, Jesus responded with what I see as a theological, spiritual foundation for accepting our limitations but still doing what we can. He said, "Leave her alone, she has done what she can, she has affirmed her love for me the best she knows how." He foretold that this act of love would go down through history as her memorial. *

Several years ago, Dr. Dan Whitaker, pastor of my parents' church, and my home church as a young boy, commenting on this story pointed out there were a number of things this woman could not do; she was limited in many ways but she did not let what she could not do keep her from what she could do. He took this as a theological foundation for doing what we can and leaving the rest up to faith, thus finding peace in spite of our limitations. **

In summary and in conclusion (for now) it is important to recognize and accept what we as parents of troubled young adults can and cannot do. I feel this dynamic is best communicated and understood by the prayer attributed to Reinhold Niebuhr better known as the Serenity Prayer: "God grant us the serenity to accept the things we cannot change, the courage to change the things we can, and the wisdom to know the difference."***

Take care.

The Reader's Page

_____

_____

_____

_____

_____

_____

_____

_____

_____

_____

_____

_____

_____

_____

_____

_____

_____

_____

_____

_____

_____

_____

_____

A Word About These Serious Economic Times

As this book is about to go to press, we are experiencing some of the most serious economic problems in my 69 years. Because of this situation, it is even more important that we as parents of problematic young adults take care of ourselves, especially in the area of finances. As I mentioned in Chapter 3, entitled *Problematic Issues* one of the most serious problems our young adults have is in the area of financial responsibility. Because of the present state of affairs in our national and local economy – particularly the loss of jobs and high unemployment – our young adults might not now be able to get a job even if they wanted to.

There are two issues I would like to speak to as it relates to this particular economic situation. First, I cannot emphasize enough the need to consider the concepts and ideas I have set forth in this book. As indeed the flight attendants tell us before we take off – 'If problems arise on board the aircraft and you are traveling with children, put your oxygen mask on first'. Secondly, because the situation is beyond both our and our troubled young adult's control, we must take this into consideration when applying the concepts and ideas in this book. Am I saying disregard everything we have been discussing? Of course not.What I am suggesting for our consideration is what I was referring to on *The Reader's Page* , and that is, "This approach to parenting troubled young adults 18 years and older is dynamic in that one can add to or take away from it as needed, conditional upon the circumstance at any given time".

List of Healthy Coping Concepts

Notes

Dedications

Page 7 – *AARP Bulletin,* December 2007, 6.

Introduction

Page 15 – John Claypool, *Mending the Heart* (Salt Lake City, UT: Cowley Publications, 1999)

Page 15 – John Claypool, *Tracks of a Fellow Struggler* (New Orleans: Insight Press, 1995)

Chapter 2

Page 30 – Margaret Mahler, *Modern Synopsis of Psychiatry, IV* by Harold Kapla and Benjamin Saddock (Baltimore, MD: Williams and Williams, 1985) 2.

Chapter 4

Page 48 – Erik Erikson, *Modern Synopsis of Psychiatry, IV* by Harold Kaplan and Benjamin Saddock (Baltimore, MD: Williams and Williams, 1985) 89- 92.

Page 55 – D.W. Winnicott, *What is Psychoanalysis? The Institute of Psychoanalysis?* (London, England: Balliere, Tindell and Cassell, 1968)

Page 60 – Unknown Author (PCR Anger Management Workbook, 2001) 47.

Page 61 – John Bradshaw, *Bradshaw on the Family* (Deerfield Beach, FL: Health Communications, Inc., 1988) 168.

Page 62 – Elisabeth Kubler-Ross, *On Death and Dying* (New York, NY: The Macmillan Company, 1969) 112.

Page 90 – *Amplified Bible,* Isaiah 1:18 (Grand Rapids, MI: Zondervon Publishers, 1965) 762.

Page 91 – *Aesop Fable's* (New York, NY: Barnes and Noble Classics, 2003).

Page 97 – Sigmund Freud, *Freud-A life for Our Tines* by Peter Gay (New York, NY, W.W. Norton and Co., 1988)164

Page 97 – Joseph Fletcher, *Situational Ethics, The New Morality* (Presbyterian Publishing Corporation: Louisville, KY, 1966)

Page 100 – *Aesop Fable's* (New York, NY: Barnes and Noble Classics, 2003)

Page 101 – Erik Erikson, *Modern Synopsis of Psychiatry, IV* by Harold Kaplan and Benjamin Saddock (Baltimore, MD: Williams and Williams, 1985) 89-90.

Page 105 – John Patton, *Is Human Forgiveness Possible?* (Nashville, TN: Abington Press, 1985)

Page 106 – John Claypool, *Mending the Heart* (Salt Lake City, UT: Cowley Publications, 1999)

Page 107 – Sigmund Freud, *A Primer of Freudian Psychology* by Calvin S. Hall (New York, NY: Mentor Books, 1954) 22-31.

Page 116 – Virginia Satir, *Conjoint Family Therapy* (Palo Alto, CA: Science and Behavior Books, 1967) 2.

Page 117 – Kathy Peel, *Family for Life* (New York, NY: McGraw Hill, 2003)

Chapter 6

Page 128 – Mr. Art Linkletter, *The Larry King Live TV Show*, CNN, 2003

Page 131 – *Amplified Bible*, Luke 15:11-32 (Grand Rapids, MI: Zondervan Publishers, 1965) 112-113.

Chapter 9

Page 149 – Charlie Shedd, *Then God Created Grandparents and It was Very Good* (New York, NY: Doubleday Publishers, 1976)

Chapter 12

Page 168 – Gloria and William J. Gaither, Hymn - *Because He Lives* (Phoenix, AZ Praised Him Sound Track Publishers, 1971)

Page 170 – Robert Havighurst, *Human Development and Education* (New York, NY: McKay, 1953) 5.

Page 170 – *Amplified Bible*, John 5:6 (Grand Rapids, MI: Zondervan Publishers, 1965) 139.

Page 174 – Joseph Campbell with Bill Moyers, *The Power of Myth* (New York, NY: Doubleday Publishers, 1988) xiii.

Page 175 – *Amplified Bible*, Mark 14:3-9 (Grand Rapids, MI: Zondervan Publishers, 1965) 121.

Page 175 – Dan Whitaker, Previous Pastor of Westside Church, Gainsville, FL

Page 175 – Reinhold Niebuhr, *The Serenity Prayer*, Edited by Robert McAfee Brown (New Haven, CT: Yale University Press, 1987)

Back Cover – Janet G. Woititz, *Adult Children of Alcoholics*, (Deerfield Beach, FL: Health Communications Inc., 1983) xxvii-xxviii.

Glossary Of Old And New Words And Terms

(As Used In This Book)

<u>Autonomy</u> – The ability of a person to self-govern as opposed to be governed by another

<u>Baby Boomer</u> – A person born between the years of 1946-1964 (plus or minus)

<u>Boomercare</u> –When a parent is taking care of oneself

<u>Boomer Co-deparent</u> – A baby boomer or any parent who has a codependent relationship with his/her problematic young adult, 18 years old or older

<u>Boomer Co-deparents' Alanonymous Support Group</u> - A support group for parents of troubled/ problematic young adults with the goals in mind of both taking care of oneself and trying to help the young adult

<u>Blended Family</u> – A family where at least one parent is a step parent

Catastrophise – Making a mountain out of a mole hill

Codependant – An unhealthy dependency of two people on each other

Emancipation Age – The age when young adults are legally responsible for themselves (for our purpose in this book age 18)

Empowerment – The ability to have the primary authority in our own life

Enabling – Attitudes and actions that a parent has that hurts not helps his/her irresponsible young adult

Enmeshed – An unhealthy emotional closeness that a parent and their young adult has which makes it difficult to see the boundary that separates the two of them

<u>Entitlement</u> – The belief that one is not only special (which we all are) but extra special (which we are not); and because one feels extra special is therefore deserving of extra special treatment

<u>Interpersonal</u> – The interaction, influence and relationship one person has with another

<u>Intrapersonal</u> – The internal thoughts and feelings of any given individual

<u>Narcissism</u> – An unhealthy and unrealistic love for oneself

<u>Pandemic</u> – This is a problem that is effecting families in all 50 states

<u>Parentification</u> – This is the concept that a parent requires their child (of any age) to live life in such

a way that the parent is being taken care of by the child i.e. keep the parent happy

<u>Pleasure Principle</u> – The seeking of immediate gratification by avoiding pain and seeking pleasure

<u>Reality Principle</u> – The ability to delay gratification to achieve a desired goal

<u>Separation – Individuation Process</u> – The process of emotional maturation that goes on with a child from birth to age 3+, especially including the relationship with his/her primary care- giver, that leads to a sense of one's own identity

<u>Troubled Young Adult</u> – A seriously irresponsible or problematic young adult

About the Author

Hi, my name is Murphy and I am a recovering co-deparent!

I am the oldest of three brothers. My father was an air conditioner mechanic and my mother was a full-time homemaker. I was born in 1944, and raised in Gainesville, Florida.

After being graduated from the University of Florida, I did my masters degree at Southern Seminary in Louisville, Kentucky, and attained my doctoral degree in Pastoral Counseling at Vanderbilt University in Nashville, Tennessee, finishing in 1972.

For several years I served on staff of two local churches emphasizing care and counseling. Following this, I went to Georgia Baptist Hospital where I completed a one year internship and a two year residency in Pastoral Care and Counseling.

Since 1984, I have had a full-time counseling practice and am licensed as a Professional Counselor, Mental Health Service Provider and Pastoral Therapist. I have a private counseling practice in McMinnville, Tennessee, (near Nashville) and am the senior therapist on staff at the Christian Counseling Center in Dalton, Georgia. Also, I am a Fellow in the American Association of Pastoral Counselors (AAPC).

My wife, (a retired school teacher of 30 years, now my office manager), and I live on a small farm in McMinnville, at the foot of the Cumberland Mountain Range, and enjoy our blended family, especially our six grandchildren and our hobbies. Dianne is an avid flower and vegetable gardener and an up-and-coming artist. I am an amateur farmer.

<u>Other Books Written by the Author</u>

Are you kidding me? One is enough!!

The following information is available for scheduling the author for workshops, conference presentations or to purchase additional copies of this book.

Dr. Murphy C. Martin, LPC
PO Box 931
Mc Minnville, TN 37110
or
<u>murphycmartin@blomand.net</u>
or
Visit us at <u>www.murphycmartin.com</u>
or
(931) 473-8279

21606005R00109

Made in the USA
Columbia, SC
20 July 2018